PRAISE FOR *GLORY IN ALL THINGS*

"In this beautiful study, Gushurst-Moore compels us to ask the right questions about the present and future prospects for humane and Christian education, while leading us at the same time to consider anew those enduring foundations in both nature and Catholic tradition from which authentic renewal must spring."

— **RYAN N. S. TOPPING**, Academic Dean of Newman Theological College, Edmonton, and author of *Renewing the Mind: A Reader in the Philosophy of Catholic Education*

"André Gushurst-Moore sets out a vision for education in which the assumption is not so much (as some say) that we need a new Benedict, but that we need to be deeply re-acquainted with the original one, whose pattern of education integrated study, work, leisure, and prayer (liturgy and *lectio divina* especially). The goal, as our author sees it, is supernatural transformation (*conversatio morum*) and the nourishment of the moral life; and it is gratifying that he stresses also the importance of serious study of visual art and images in both traditional and modern expressions — for example, photography — as a vital component. He makes the telling point that few students can be expected to follow this path unless they are guided by the example of teachers striving for the same end themselves."

— **DAVID CLAYTON**, Provost, Pontifex University, and author of *The Way of Beauty: Liturgy, Education, and Inspiration for Family, School, and College*

"This book is an enchanting read. It sets out the hallmarks of a Benedictine education with such erudition that one comes away feeling hopeful for the future. It is consoling to know that in the field of Catholic education there are still some familiar with the cultural treasure of the Christian centuries and its Benedictine graces. If the ideas presented in this work are taken seriously, we may well harbor hope of winning the culture wars of our time. As the author says, we don't so much need a new St. Benedict as people with the courage to actually put the ideas of the old St. Benedict into practice."

— **TRACEY ROWLAND**, St. John Paul II Chair of Theology, University of Notre Dame (Australia)

"In an age of radical relativism and secular fundamentalism the very future of authentic education is under threat. André Gushurst-Moore unmasks the flaws of modern education and reveals the marks of what constitutes an education grounded in eternal life-giving verities. He outlines the priceless inheritance of Western civilization, and shows, especially, how the inheritance of the Benedictine tradition can be passed on to future generations."

— **JOSEPH PEARCE**, Director of Book Publishing at the Augustine Institute, editor of the *St. Austin Review*

"A wonderful sense of relief follows upon a reading of André Gushurst-Moore's work on Benedictine education — for he has patiently walked us through the ancient yet still living wisdom flowing from fifteen centuries of this classical education. He reintroduces to us the Western educational tradition, which offers as its perspective, in the words of Evelyn Waugh, the 'most long-sighted view it is possible to take' — the view of the Gospel itself, in which we are helped to find the glory of God in all things. Gushurst-Moore's work, both visionary and practical, will greatly assist us both in regaining this authentic Catholic perspective on education and in learning how to incarnate the central Benedictine virtues and practices in our educational endeavors."

— **PETROC WILLEY**, Director of the Catechetical Institute and the Office of Catechetics, Franciscan University of Steubenville

"In this ground-breaking, profound, and counter-cultural book, the author demonstrates that the Benedictine ethos and its pedagogical principles offer crucial lessons for all Catholic educational institutions facing the challenges of the Modern Age. In eight chapters dealing with Beginnings, Spirit, Transformations, Leadership, Learning, Curriculum, Co-Curriculum or (Service), and Living, the author achieves a 'tour de force.' The wisdoms of Benedictine education and ethos are made visible by this book — wisdoms crucial for the future of Catholic education worldwide. *Glory in All Things* is not for Benedictines only, but for the world."

— **GERALD GRACE**, Centre for Research and Development in Catholic Education, St. Mary's Catholic University

"An intelligent, well-written, thought-provoking book that applies Christian realism to education in a way that is challenging, wise, inspirational, and full of hope. The author renders education—as illuminated by the Benedictine ethos—attractive, relevant, credible, life-enhancing, and community-building. In contrast to educational approaches that are too narrow, and constricted by cultural assumptions that stifle openness to the transcendent, Gushurst-Moore advocates teaching, learning, and leadership that deepens our appreciation of personhood and stretches the spirit, rather than one fixated on accumulating qualifications and preparing for market competitiveness."

— **JOHN SULLIVAN**, Professor Emeritus, Liverpool Hope University

"In the broadest sense, André Gushurst-Moore here unpacks the Benedict Option—and spells out what its application might mean in every school, home, and life. He shares his love and knowledge of the *Rule* of St. Benedict, but also draws on the wisdom of John Henry Newman, G. K. Chesterton, C. S. Lewis, Alasdair MacIntyre, Pope Benedict XVI, and many others. Any parent who worries about the formation their child is receiving should read *Glory in All Things* and encourage their child's school to draw upon a tried and tested tradition that provides a map and compass to navigate the hazards and crises of life—which is precisely what this marvelous book offers."

— **DAVID ALTON**, Professor the Lord Alton, Independent Crossbench Peer

Glory in All Things

Glory in All Things

St Benedict
&
Catholic Education
Today

ANDRÉ GUSHURST-MOORE

Angelico Press

First published in the USA
by Angelico Press 2020
Copyright © André Gushurst-Moore 2020

For information, address:
Angelico Press, Ltd.
169 Monitor St.
Brooklyn, NY 11222
www.angelicopress.com

paper 978-1-62138-506-6
cloth 978-1-62138-507-3
ebook 978-1-62138-508-0

Book and cover design
by Michael Schrauzer

For Bruna,
*historian, medical herbalist, teacher, poet
(a Hildegard of our days), beloved wife, and
beloved mother of our grown-up children,
Alexandra, Christian, and Josephine.*

Quisquis ergo ad patriam cælestem festinas,
hanc minimam inchoationis regulam
descriptam adiuvante Christo perfice
Regula Benedicti, 73:8

CONTENTS

INTRODUCTION

A TIME FOR RENEWAL

On April 1, 2005, the day before Pope John Paul II died, then-Cardinal Joseph Ratzinger gave a lecture at Subiaco in Italy. Subiaco is the place where the young Benedict of Nursia retired to a cave, having left his studies in Rome, about the year 500 A D. The cave of Subiaco is in some ways the symbolic womb from which Christian Europe emerged, under the extensive and long-lasting tutelage of St Benedict and his Rule. No wonder, then, that it was at Subiaco, in 2005, that Cardinal Ratzinger gave such profound consideration to the current state of the inheritance passed down to modern Europe from St Benedict. The cardinal noted the departure from the ways of the past, and from Christianity, of modern science and technology, political constitutions, ethical norms, social expectations with regard to marriage and the family, and religious observance. He concluded: "Above all, that of which we are in need at this moment in history are men who, through an enlightened and lived faith, render God credible in this world....We need men who have their gaze directed to God, to understand true humanity. We need men whose intellects are enlightened by the light of God, and whose hearts God opens, so that their intellects can speak to the intellects of others, and so that their hearts are able to open up to the hearts of others."[1] A society that recognizes "true humanity," argues Cardinal Ratzinger, needs to be rebuilt on the basis of faith, a renewal of the inner life of man, before the wider life of society will rise anew: "Only through men who have been touched by God, can God come near to men. We need men like Benedict of Norcia, who at a time

1   Cardinal Joseph Ratzinger, "On Europe's Crisis of Culture" (lecture, Subiaco, Italy, April 1, 2005). https://www.catholiceducation.org/en/culture/catholic-con-tributions/cardinal-ratzinger-on-europe-s-crisis-of-culture.html.

of dissipation and decadence, plunged into the most profound solitude, succeeding, after all the purifications he had to suffer, to ascend again to the light, to return and to found Montecasino [sic], the city on the mountain that, with so many ruins, gathered together the forces from which a new world was formed."[2] The present book considers the implications for education arising from this central need of our culture today, and how schools especially can provide a means for young people to be touched by God, and then come near to others.

Cardinal Ratzinger was perhaps recalling in his speech the words of the Catholic philosopher Alasdair MacIntyre in his book *After Virtue*, but he must also have been aware of the importance of St Benedict of Nursia (or Norcia, to use its current name) to Pope John Paul II,[3] and to Pope Paul VI who, in 1964, designated St Benedict the Patron of Europe. More recently, the American journalist Rod Dreher has seen St Benedict as the model of how Christians should respond to a post-Christian society, and Dreher's book *The Benedict Option* has generated much discussion and debate. Dreher comes to the bleak conclusion that "the public square has been lost,"[4] the final blow being the U. S. Supreme Court's *Obergefell* decision allowing a constitutional right to same-sex marriage. Dreher sees this as a defining moment, and one that substantiates Pope Benedict's observation in 2012 of a spiritual crisis overtaking the West, the most serious since the fall of the Roman Empire at the end of the fifth century. The West has now become, says Dreher, a "blasted heath of atomization, fragmentation and unbelief."[5] What, we might wonder, will be the likely result of this spiritual crisis?

In Dreher's view there will be more social instability, and an ever-cruder culture of vulgarity, desensitizing and dehumanizing;

---

2   Ibid.

3   See his address to the monks of Monte Cassino (May 18, 1979), and his message to the Abbot of Subiaco on the feast of St Benedict, Patron of Europe (July 7, 1999).

4   Rod Dreher, *The Benedict Option* (New York: Sentinel Press, 2017), 9.

5   Ibid., 45.

the medical-industrial complex will increase its hold on human life, especially at its beginning and end; the hostility to the Christian religion will grow, and Islam will become further embedded in social and political life; politics will become more venal and life generally about money-making, career development, and insulating oneself against the breakdown in civility; the media will also become more vulgar and reflective of declining standards for what is acceptable in the public sphere; education will be increasingly focused on gaining qualifications rather than acquiring wisdom; the traditional family will be the exception rather than the norm for children, except among Islamic families; there will be ever-greater separation of the majority of the population from nature and the natural world; populism will appeal to ever-lower instincts; and plutocracy will move farther from the reach of the civil and criminal law, which itself will be farther removed from the law of God and of nature. In such an atmosphere of civil decline, there must be, Dreher suggests, a withdrawal by Christians into, as it were, a Subiaco condition, to make almost self-sufficient base communities that insulate themselves as much as possible against the effects of a hostile culture.

Even if we might consider Dreher's "survivalist" program polemical rather than well-balanced, his analysis of the contemporary Western culture is powerful in its effect and incisive in its clarity. In one sense, he is simply taking the implications of the New Evangelization seriously, in showing how post-Christian Western culture has become increasingly anti-Christian and (from the religious perspective) anti-human and is in need of a reawakening to the truths of the Gospel. Dreher seems to have little faith in the capacity of the culture to adjust itself — perhaps, one might think, on the basis of common sense — through sheer resilience of human nature. It may be that the liberal democracy that emerged regnant from the Second World War and the following Cold War has changed into something that is authoritarian, hubristic, dogmatic, and self-sufficient in it approach to social order, a liberalism that has shed its Christian roots to become militantly secular. In suggesting this, Dreher echoes an earlier critic of liberalism in state and Church: "Yet speak I must; for the times are very evil, yet no one speaks against them."[6] Thus said St John Henry Newman, then a young Anglican priest, in 1833. Indeed, the Church has faced the world in a battle for its survival on many occasions in its history. In *The Everlasting Man*, G. K. Chesterton wrote of "The Five Deaths of the Faith": "At least five times, therefore, with the Arian and the Albigensian, with the Humanist sceptic, after Voltaire and after Darwin, the Faith has to all appearance gone to the dogs. In each of these five cases it was the dog that died."[7] Moreover, from the perspective of continuing tension between state and Church, between God and Caesar, the first Good Friday began the pattern of catastrophes facing believers. Thus the model of decay and renewal, within and outside the Church, seems to be with us always; it is not a matter of a consistent decline from the High Middle Ages, as Dreher suggests. The history of the Church tells us both that things might become very much worse for Christians and that they can become much better.

A DISENCHANTED PRESENT

Whether or not one agrees with Rod Dreher's analysis, or with his conclusion in favor of a policy of disengagement from a hopelessly vitiated culture, it seems beyond dispute that the West is moving into a near future that is to all intents and purposes post-Christian. The authority of recent popes, among others, supports such a view. But the myth of a decline from a Golden Age is an old one, predating Christianity, and we must be careful about substituting for the secular myth of increasing progress and liberty (the "Whig interpretation of history") an equal and opposite myth of irreversible decline. The times may indeed be very evil, but history does not work through iron laws of determinism. As the Catholic historian Christopher Dawson put it: "To the Christian

---

6   John Henry Newman, *Tract One* (Didcot, Oxon: The Rocket Press, 1985), 15.

7   G. K. Chesterton, *The Everlasting Man* (London: Hodder and Stoughton, 1925), 296.

the hidden principle of the life of culture and the fate of nations and civilizations must always be found in the heart of man and in the hand of God. There is no limit to the efficacy of faith and to the influence of these acts of spiritual decision which are ultimately the response of particular men to God's call, as revealed in particular historical and personal circumstances."[8] Certainly, such a man was St Benedict, but such are all Christians called to be.

Perhaps we should emphasize less the need for a new St Benedict (as MacIntyre famously suggested) than a need for something like the old St Benedict's approach to living the Gospel. St Benedict did not set out, we can assume, to save Western civilization; this was a by-product of the Benedictine approach to daily conversion of heart in those committed to living the Christian life. If, then, we take a less disenchanted approach to the present than Dreher does, and we see the present, wherever in it we find ourselves, as being the womb of the future, the Benedictine approach can be a source of renewal and of hope. The times are very evil, but also full of much good, and Christians should not, just because they live in a disenchanted culture, become themselves the means of disenchantment. Rather, we can say in faith that in the here and now there is glory in all things — if people have eyes to see.

The cultural disenchantment that came with the Enlightenment may be a significant source of the disenchanted spirit that possesses our culture today. Disenchantment works in the hearts and minds of people such that the glory that inheres both in the outer reality of the world and in the interior lives of individuals becomes invisible to them. It is the task of education to challenge this false view of reality, but there is a widespread view today that mainstream education, whether state-maintained or independent, is failing to do what education should. Dreher is clear on this point: "Today our education system fills students' heads with facts, with no higher aspiration than success in worldly endeavor.

---

8 Christopher Dawson, in *Christianity and European Culture: Selections from the Work of Christopher Dawson,* ed. Gerald J. Russello (Washington, D.C.: CUA Press, 1998), 7.

Since the High Middle Ages, the pursuit of knowledge for its own sake has been slowly separated from the pursuit of virtue. Today the break is clean."[9] Dreher advocates an alternative education grounded in Scripture and the history of Western civilization, through homeschooling or new classical Christian schools; all this would involve a rigorous selection of course content and schooling environment. It is an approach to the problem that involves disengagement from an atmosphere of disenchantment in mainstream education, with the assumption that a better educational atmosphere can indeed be established in the home or in small, independent Christian schools.

A different perspective on education is provided by Tony Little, the former headmaster of one of the world's leading independent schools, Eton College, near Windsor, in England. Little has also lamented the current cultural assumptions about education, as being a utilitarian, exam-results-driven machine for worldly success: "It is a sad thing; where once men spoke of the Age of Enlightenment, we now live in the Age of Measurement."[10] Furthermore, Little criticizes the absence of *wonder* in the inspection rubrics for "spiritual, moral, social and cultural" (to use the inspectors' category) education in British schools. He opposes the atheist biologist and polemicist Richard Dawkins's insistence on explaining the wonder of the natural world in scientific terms alone, and posits, instead of *material* humanism, a *spiritual* humanism as an outlook to develop in the young.

There has come to be, then, a certain disenchantment in the world of education, reflective of that in the wider culture, which includes not only the perspectives of a radical Orthodox Christian and a liberal English independent school headmaster, but also those of politicians of every stripe, teachers, parents, and pupils. Even leaders in the world of business and commerce, whom one might expect to have a more sympathetic view of the

---

9 Dreher, 148.
10 Tony Little, *An Intelligent Person's Guide to Education* (London: Bloomsbury, 2015), 16.

utilitarian drift in education, frequently note that job applicants lack *character*, for all their paper qualifications, and are thus not easily employable. In different ways, and from different religious (and non-religious) perspectives, there is a strong sense in Western society that education is failing to develop in the young the most important human qualities, the deepest areas of human life. However much more our society demands in terms of Science, Technology, Engineering and Mathematics (the so-called STEM subjects), it appears that it is most lacking in the deeper need to educate the human person, with all the cultural, moral, religious, and spiritual implications that go with such a conclusion. There is far too little direction of the young in what is essential for human development; curricula allow for wide choice among subjects of apparently equal value — or none at all, depending on the subjective tastes and whims of particular pupils and their parents. Schools lack confidence and purpose in giving moral direction, except where ideological guidance is imposed upon them by the coercive State. The best teachers continue to work as well as they can in such an atmosphere, loyal to their vocation, and knowing that teaching is about the love of learning and a life willingly shared with pupils.

This is good, practical wisdom, but there is a need also for a larger vision of the aims of education to sustain individual human beings, and a humane society, into the future. Where is such a vision to be found?

AN EDUCATION FOR THE AGES

Eton College (or, to give it its full original name, "The King's College of Our Lady of Eton besides Wyndsor") represents world-class excellence in a highly desirable form of secondary education: the English boarding or "public" school. (Actually, these schools are "private" in the sense of being reliant on their own sources of income, through either fees or endowments, but the word *public* originally signified a charitable openness and a level of public regulation, free of private proprietorship.) Founded in 1440 by King

Henry VI, Eton not only has Catholic roots, but it also reflects the monastic origins of Christian education in England, which had been Catholic for a thousand years before the sixteenth-century Reformation. The school which claims to be the oldest continuously operating school in the world is also in England: The King's School, Canterbury, founded in 597 A D by St Augustine of Canterbury as part of his mission from Pope St Gregory the Great to convert the pagan Anglo-Saxons. The foundations of St Augustine's abbey lie today on the grounds of The King's School, which was re-founded as such by Henry VIII after the dissolution of the monasteries in the sixteenth century. In terms of ethos, the English public schools can be seen still to possess something of their ancient Christian and monastic inheritance in emphasizing the education of the "whole person." Behind what Tony Little calls "the liberal British holistic tradition"[11] in education runs over fifteen hundred years of Christianity in the British Isles.

Little also makes the conventional link in British independent schools between a "liberal education" (originally, one based in the liberal arts) and a liberal approach to religion and spirituality, so that humanity is not sacrificed to religion: "Creeds constrain. The risk for formal religion is that it becomes a thing in itself, and is seen as such by the young, not a channel for the spirit. Creeds tend to be written after the charismatic individual has gone. It is a challenge for young people to consider whether Jesus would have wished for a formal creed at all."[12] Little's approach might seem to articulate something even more formless than what Rod Dreher calls Moralistic Therapeutic Deism (MTD); to Catholics, creeds create freedom. Nonetheless, there is a wisdom in both Little's and Dreher's approaches, however divergent they might initially appear. Is it possible to consider a form of education that is authentically Christian (as Dreher would wish) and that also addresses, in an expansive and inclusive way, the full needs and potential of the human person (as Little desires)?

11 Ibid., 30.
12 Ibid., 148.

The present book seeks to do that insofar as it attempts to describe the oldest form of Catholic education, and one that has touched almost every part of Christian European culture, as well as its extension into the wider West and other parts of the Christian world. The monastic and Benedictine tradition continues not only in some of the ancient European schools, many of which are no longer Catholic, but also in Benedictine schools founded in the nineteenth-century efflorescence of monasticism that continued into the twentieth century, especially in Europe and the Americas. Today, there are nearly 200 Benedictine and Cistercian schools worldwide, all inspired by the Rule of St Benedict, and educating some 130,000 students, working in a variety of funding models, and educating young people from a variety of religious and economic backgrounds.[13] Such schools, and the whole Benedictine tradition in learning and education, are emblematic of wider themes in Catholic and Christian education, particularly as they provide a concrete example of a Christian humanist perspective. Furthermore, it is not supposed here that education can exist unto itself, or be meaningfully considered except in relation to the wider culture in which it works, and of which it can provide a critique. It is taken for granted that a Catholic and Benedictine education depends on a particular philosophy of life, and that this philosophy of life no longer enjoys an "established" or conventionally accepted place in Western culture and institutions. The term "Benedictine education," while implying Catholicity, refers here to a particular educational approach and tradition (like Jesuit education) within the wider educational project of the Catholic Church.

The first half of this book considers the general perspectives behind Benedictine education, including in its historical context, and also includes the Benedictine approach to leadership, as important for schools as for other enterprises inspired by the Rule of St Benedict. The second half of the book considers the approach to learning and education that might usefully be seen

---

13   More broadly, there are today some 58 million students in Catholic schools and colleges, up from 31 million in 1971.

as being within the Benedictine tradition, but also including other perspectives within the Catholic tradition. The conclusion looks forward to ways in which the tradition of humanistic education may be of value in the years ahead, as the idea of what it is to be human becomes more contested, and new challenges arise for those who seek an education for a life worth living. References are made to works from beyond the Catholic world, in a way that is intended to reflect the wider culture, but which also reflects the vagaries of the present writer's reading and predilections. It is hoped that the book will be of interest and usefulness not only to those who teach and study in Benedictine and other Catholic schools and colleges, but also to parents of those students, and anyone interested in the foundations of a Christian and humanist education.

In Evelyn Waugh's short story "Scott-King's Modern Europe" (1946), the eponymous hero is an aging classics teacher in a conventional English boarding school; it is set in the writer's present, that is, the end of the Second World War, with its deadening privations and political upheavals. Boys in the school are increasingly choosing "modern" subjects, like Economic History and Physics, rather than the "classics" of Latin and ancient Greek. After some unlikely comic adventures in a fictional Eastern European state over a summer vacation, adventures which serve to confirm Scott-King in his very low opinion of the modern world, he returns to school for the coming term, beginning in September. The headmaster asks to see Scott-King, to give him the sad news that there will be even fewer classical students in the coming academic year than previously. "I deplore it as much you do," says the headmaster: "But what are we to do? Parents are not interested in producing the 'complete man' any more. They want to qualify their boys for jobs in the modern world. You can hardly blame them, can you?" "Oh, yes," said Scott-King. "I can and do." But, the headmaster tells Scott-King, there may come a time when there are no pupils at all for the classics classroom; perhaps Scott-King might like to teach economic history? Scott-King refuses. The headmaster asks, "Then what do you intend to do?" Scott-King replies: "If you approve, head master, I will stay as I am here as long as any boy wants to read the classics. I think it would be very wicked indeed to do anything to fit a boy for the modern world." The headmaster replies: "It's a short-sighted view, Scott-King." But Scott-King concludes: "There, head master, with all respect, I differ from you profoundly. I think it the most long-sighted view it is possible to take."[14]

Scott-King, utterly disenchanted with the world, retreats into his subject. Whether or not it would be positively wicked to prepare the young for life in the modern world, the present book seeks to promote an education that would enable them to be critical of it, such that they can come to some appreciation, and understanding, of the longest view it is possible to take. That view, longer even than the classical one, is the Gospel vision, in which there is, as St Benedict suggests, glory in all things.

---

14 "Scott-King's Modern Europe," passim. In Evelyn Waugh, *Work Suspended and Other Stories* (London: Penguin, 1982).

CHAPTER 1

Beginnings

REMAKING THE WORLD

In 529 A D, St Benedict founded an abbey at Monte Cassino, a natural fortress some eighty miles southeast of Rome. It was to be sacked or destroyed many times, first by the Lombards in 580, subsequently by the Saracens, then by earthquake, then by Napoleon — and then it was dissolved in 1866. Its most recent destruction was on February 15, 1944, when American bombers dropped 1,400 tons of high explosives on the abbey. The action was part of the second of four battles for the site, battles that culminated in an Allied victory, making way for the advance on German-occupied Rome. Between January 17 and May 18, 1944, the attacks on Monte Cassino cost 55,000 Allied casualties and 20,000 German. For the Allies, the fighting was comparable in its slaughter to Verdun or Passchendaele in the First World War; for the Germans, it recalled Stalingrad. The bombing on February 15, however, succeeded in killing 230 Italian civilians, and allowed the German forces nearby to occupy the ruins, where before they had agreed not to use the abbey for military purposes.

It was, said the Cardinal Secretary of State, Luigi Maglione, "a colossal blunder... a piece of gross stupidity."[1] It is redolent of the chaotic nature of war so memorably pictured in the third volume of Evelyn Waugh's *Sword of Honour* trilogy, where he writes, "The allies had lately much impeded their advance by the destruction of Monte Cassino, but the price of this sacrilege was being paid by the infantry of the front line."[2] Waugh was more aware than most

---

1 David Hapgood and David Richardson, *Monte Cassino* (New York, NY: Berkley Books, 1986), 244.
2 Evelyn Waugh, *Unconditional Surrender* (London: Penguin, 1974), 168.

1

of the irony involved when, in the Second World War, Christian
soldiers on the Allied side were destroying churches in the defense
of what Churchill had called "Christian civilization." The irony
was nowhere more obvious than at Monte Cassino. In this place,
out of the chaotic uncertainty and casual cruelty of barbarian
rule, St Benedict, one of the last of the ancient Romans, had built
a fortress to God, an outpost of what was to become a new Rome,
the Christian West that endures (barely, perhaps) to this day.

St Benedict was named Patron of Europe in 1964, by Pope
Paul VI,[3] when on October 24 of that year he re-consecrated the
abbey church, now rebuilt according to the original plans. It was at
Cassino, which had endured in its own body the total war of the
twentieth century, that the Supreme Pontiff would bestow on Benedict six titles. Benedict, said Pope Paul (in Latin), was Messenger
of Peace, Architect of Unity, Teacher of Civilization and Culture,
Herald of the Christian Religion, Founder of Western Monasticism and — the new title — Patron of the Whole of Europe. The
historical context of Pope Paul's act was not only reconstruction
after the Second World War, but also the burgeoning European
project that would become the European Union, part of post-war
attempts to ensure that never again would there be a European
conflict — always at the deepest level a civil war. Today, it seems
that the European political project must be reassessed, and in
that, as Pope Emeritus Benedict XVI has taught us, St Benedict
must be our guide.

Pope Paul grounded his vision of the Benedictine charism in
the word *peace* (*pax*), which often marks the door of a Benedictine
monastery. The message of St Benedict, Messenger of Peace (*Pacis
Nuntius*) for his own time, is also one for ours, when the world,
including a Europe increasingly scarred by Islamist terrorism, is
undergoing a deep civilizational crisis. Now, just as it once did amid
the disorder of the decline and fall of the Roman Empire, monastic
living under the Rule of St Benedict made a certain kind of life

---

3   Paul VI, *Pacis Nuntius*. http://w2.vatican.va/content/paul-vi/la/apost_let-
ters/documents/hf_p-vi_apl_19641024_pacis-nuntius.html.

possible, as well as providing a sign for the local world around the monastery. "Consider this," says the monastic community; "if you think in your heart that this way is of value, how might you live your own lives, within or outside the cloister?" St Benedict's is a way for life in a world of death, the art and craft of making a place of refreshment, of light and peace — a symbol of heaven.

St Benedict, says Pope Paul, is also Architect of Unity (*Unitatis Effector*). Benedict and his monasteries were no respecters of persons. Roman nobility, immigrant barbarians, rich, poor, slave, free — all were equal under the Rule. The only order is the seniority determined by date of entry into the monastic life; the only supremacy is that of Christ, in the elected fatherhood of the abbot, or motherhood of the abbess. Nearly all the countries of modern Europe have or have had Benedictine communities, and Pope Paul sought the blessing of Benedict on the post-war movement towards European unity, or "fraternal bonds among the nations of Europe," as the pope put it. Although Benedict himself sought solitude and prayer, rather than great religious or political projects, it was — as we shall see — the spread of the centers of monasticism that remade the cultural unity of the West after the disintegration of Roman rule in the sixth century.

It is this cultural unity that fosters the humanity of Europe, more so than factitious and transient political structures, and it is this Benedictine achievement that Pope Paul acknowledges in the third of the titles he applies to Benedict: "Teacher of Civilization and Culture (*Civilis Cultus Magister*)." The sons and daughters of Benedict took with them "the cross, the book and the plough" — symbols of the cultivation of the heart and the soul, the mind and the earth, that represent the integrated Benedictine ideal. The combination of scholarship with farming marks a distinctive break with the Roman decadence that Benedict saw around him. The distinction between slave and free in antiquity determined the work which a man was to do. The servile arts, lower or higher forms of manual work, were done by slaves. The liberal arts, the higher learning of grammar, rhetoric, philosophy, and the rest, were what belonged to the free man, the type of what later ages would know as the "gentleman." Although the despising of manual labor continues in our own age (would the West of today survive without "illegal" immigrant manual laborers?), Benedictine life despises nothing that is necessary, and welcomes it as a gift: "For they are not really monks unless they live by the work of their own hands, like our Fathers and the Apostles" (*Rule of St Benedict* 48:1, 8). The enormous creative potentiality of the earth was to be realized in the economic life of the Middle Ages, driven as it was by monastic houses, particularly the Cistercian.

Cultural decadence might be measured in our physical and spiritual distance from the land, and there is nothing new under the sun. Benedict had conservative Roman instincts, and surely he remembered, with so many of the best of the Romans from the earliest times to the fall of Rome's greatness, the spirit of Cincinnatus. Every Roman worth his salt was essentially a farmer, and after he did his duty to the public weal he returned — in real humility — to his home and his plough. In Benedict's Rule we see primarily a heart energized by fervent love of the Gospel, but we also hear one who thinks in the age-old language of Roman virtue: self-restraint, order, dignity, obedience, piety, and respect for fathers. If it was Cicero who coined the word *humanitas*, and Tertullian the word *Romanitas*, it was Benedict, more than anyone, who conveyed these qualities into the lives of both medievals and moderns. What we think of as kindness, refinement, civilized and cultured behavior is all wrapped up in this Roman (and Benedictine) word — *humanity*.

But in their use of the plough, the Benedictines did not neglect the book. One reason, perhaps, that there were (for example) only two universities in medieval England (as opposed, say, to the four of smaller Scotland) was that the number of great Benedictine houses of learning made universities somewhat redundant. Yet both learning and agriculture were integrated into the pattern of Christian living that was the deeper purpose of the Benedictine Rule. As Pope Paul's fourth title has it, Benedict is "Herald of the Christian religion (*Religionis Christianae Praeco*)," and this through being — the fifth title — "Founder of Western monasticism (*Monasticae Vitae in Occidente Auctor*)." Benedictine life taught the Christian Europe that was to come how to live in a self-supporting locality, a widening community of mutual help, in which we daily rely on others, and on God. More than plough and book, it is the way of the Cross that underlies all Benedictine living. In the end, as Hilaire Belloc trenchantly put it, "The Faith is Europe. And Europe is the Faith"[4]: no amount of clever political arrangement, or even a piety towards high culture or the earth itself, can endure without the Cross.

Where on the arc of progression and decay does Europe lie today? Civilization is widely understood in technical terms rather than as a quality of humane living, and the past has become just another form of entertainment. As Pope Benedict XVI has taught us, only a return to the Christian Faith will help us in the long run, on the spiritual, cultural, or political level. As we shall see, the way of St Benedict endures still, with an extraordinary resilience, most especially in Benedictine education, where it can be a vital source of rebirth for European faith and culture, beginning in the hearts of its teachers and students.

ST BENEDICT

At the end of his book *After Virtue* (1981), Alasdair MacIntyre warns against making glib parallels between our own time and that of the decline of the Roman Empire. We might remember also that since the earliest beginnings of Christianity, apocalyptic thoughts have always been with us, along with a disposition to see signs of the end. But MacIntyre admits that there are parallels between our own times and those from the beginnings of the Dark Ages to the medieval period. He notes that a distinguishing mark of the decline of Rome was that men started to abandon the moral maintenance of the whole Roman *imperium*, and to construct instead "new forms of community within which the moral life can be sustained so that both morality and civility might survive

4   Hilaire Belloc, *Europe and the Faith* (Rockford, IL: TAN, 1992), 191.

the coming ages of barbarism and darkness."[5] The new dark ages, says MacIntyre, "are already upon us," and we need to build "local forms of community within which civility and the intellectual and moral life can be sustained."[6] We must be conscious that the barbarians have "been governing us for some time," and our options are the following: nihilistic despair, waiting for the unknown, or (preferably) the renewal of what has come down to us: "We are waiting not for a Godot, but for another—doubtless very different—St Benedict."[7] Whether or not we sense that the moral order and our general social forms can no longer be expected to sustain each other, the idea that social renewal will be in local and smaller forms of community finds echoes in Catholic and other teaching in late modernity. What has been increasingly evident in the time since MacIntyre wrote the above is that such places of smaller, local community, with much expectation resting upon them, are our schools; more and more they are expected to make up for the moral deficits in the home, the workplace, and the centers of government.

What did St Benedict find in the schools of his time? The quality of Roman education towards the end of the fifth century was not what it had been. St Gregory tells us that Benedict was not impressed by either the learning or the learners he found in Rome when his parents sent him there for a conventional "liberal education": "When he found many of the students there abandoning themselves to vice, he decided to withdraw from the world he had been preparing to enter; for he was afraid that if he acquired any of its learning he would be drawn down with them to his eternal ruin."[8] While there is something classically hagiographic here, in the saint turning from the world and sacrificing a career for

5   Alasdair MacIntyre, *After Virtue: A Study in Moral Theory* (London: Duckworth, 1985), 263.

6   Ibid.

7   Ibid.

8   St Gregory the Great, *Life and Miracles of St Benedict*, trans. Odo J. Zimmerman, O.S.B. and Benedict R. Avery, O.S.B. (Collegeville, MN: Liturgical Press, 1949), 1.

God, if we read Gregory at face-value it is not so much the moral laxity of the students that Benedict turns from as the education that fails to engage their moral lives. The education sounds like, and is likely to have been, that kind promoted by the Sophists, that is, one that promoted style over content, and a certain kind of cleverness, rather than cultivating the deeper life of the mind and the heart. Benedict's "liberal education" would have started with the language arts of grammar, dialectic, and rhetoric, and in the denuded Rome of Benedict's day a literary education was most likely to have given students a facile ability to use language to get what they wanted in the marketplace or the law courts, to make a career at a time when they and their parents were fearful of their place in an increasingly uncertain world. (Such anxieties are felt by parents and students nowadays, too.)

We can imagine therefore that Benedict did not shrink from a Roman education out of mere delicacy, but because he found it insufficiently nourishing of inclinations he already possessed when he arrived in Rome. We know nothing of his home life in Nursia (the modern Norcia, a hill town in Umbria, central Italy) except that he likely came from the "gentry" (the upper-middle class), not the nobility as it is sometimes claimed. There is no reason to think that Benedict came from an aristocratic or patrician background (unlike Pope St Gregory the Great). It is possible, therefore, that he would have been familiar with an orderly life in the country, secure in his family estates, and in the manners and attitudes of an older Rome.[9] The moral life in Nursia would have been bound up with the responsibilities and duties of master and servant, and the cultivation of the land, against a backdrop of the Roman *familia* in the word's wider sense, denoting a household under a *paterfamilias*, or *dominus*. There would likely have been books there, and Benedict may well have learned much in the library of his father, in the ordered world of home, and have found

---

9   Rather than seeing in Benedict someone of undeveloped or rustic mind and taste, we might reasonably imagine in him a preference for the simpler refinement of the country over the brash utilitarianism of the city.

what was on offer in Rome disappointing and even inferior to what he had already studied. That he was sent to Rome at all confirms that his family had means. Compared to the inspiration of his Christian faith, and what he had acquired in manners and habits of life before embarking on higher education, it is not surprising that Benedict decided to head in a different direction.

That St Benedict's experience of Rome was likely to have been disappointing need not surprise us. During the second half of the fifth century A D, the population of the city had fallen from about 500,000 to only 100,000, and it was to fall further.[10] Many of the great houses were abandoned, as Rome's income from the provinces steadily fell. Wealthy families left for Constantinople. Abbot Cuthbert Butler has memorably described the wider picture of Italy in decline:

> The picture is one of decay, disorganization, and confusion perhaps without parallel in history.... Italy had become pauperized and depopulated: the ceaseless wars at home and abroad had thinned the population; the formation of huge estates worked by slave labor had crushed out the yeoman farmer class; oppressive taxation had ruined the provincial middle classes; the wholesale employment of barbarous mercenary soldiers ... established in the country an element of lawlessness and savagery. The land was devastated by famines and pestilences, till by the end of the fourth century great tracts had been reduced to deserts, the people had become demoralized and degenerate, agriculture and education had well-nigh died out, and society was corrupt to the core.[11]

Following this time came the great movement of peoples known as the barbarian invasions. The ills that Butler delineates have been

---

10   See Richard Newman, *Saint Benedict in His Time* (Abergavenny: Three Peaks Press, 2013), 23.

11   Cuthbert Butler, *Benedictine Monachism: Studies in Benedictine Life and Rule* (London: Longmans, Green and Co., 1919), 3.

seen in many places at various times since, and we can recognize them in the world of today, if not necessarily in the West. What we do know in our own day, however, is the departure of those in authority from traditional beliefs and customs, and it is of those older ways, combined with the Christian faith, that Benedictine life has always consisted. As Richard Newman has put it:

> The Roman ethical tradition, now strongly influenced by Christianity, ran parallel with the specifically Christian tradition that Benedict learnt from the scriptures and the Church fathers. What proportion of Benedict's spirituality was derived from each of these sources is impossible to say, but it seems that RB is based, in part, upon the inherited culture of its author and is not simply developed from Benedict's reading of Christian texts or borrowed from earlier monastic rules.[12]

That the best of old Rome should be bound up forever with the Catholic world owes more to St Benedict, through the dissemination of his Rule, than to any other man.

Benedict, then, nowadays a heavenly patron of students, was, in his early maturity, perhaps no great scholar. The Second Dialogue, traditionally attributed to St Gregory, describes Benedict as "*scienter nescius et sapienter indoctus*" — "learnedly ignorant and wisely uninstructed":[13] a witty but ambiguous formulation. Was St Benedict an autodidact who had made the most of his father's library? Was he naturally or blessedly wise enough to see through the limitations of Roman Sophists? Did he already know the value of such practical wisdom as a well-ordered estate would have taught him? We can know nothing of Benedict's early life for certain, but what the Rule presupposes, and subsequent Benedictine history confirms, is a preference, so far as the spiritual life is concerned, for three things more likely to be found in a country

12 Richard Newman, 69.
13 Cf. Richard Newman, 33.

place: silence, solitude, and simplicity. We should see Benedict's choice of life at Subiaco, for instance, as a vigorously positive step in the direction of the monastic life, always in its fundamentals an experience of solitude, whether it be in the strictly eremitic life or in community. Benedict was called from eremitic solitude to community on account of a perceived leadership ability, when some monks asked him to be their abbot. Benedict seems to have been still quite young when this happened, and although he was reluctant to accept the request, leadership had perhaps already been bred in him at home. What the three years as a hermit in the peace of Subiaco would have given Benedict is the chance to dwell on things both spiritual and secular, as he contemplated the ruins of Nero's palace, not far from his cave. This symbol of the ruins of Rome's greatness was also a symbol of its corruption. It was to be Benedict's calling to renew the life of Rome in the spirit of Christ.

The period we know as Rome's decline and fall was indeed a time of new beginnings. During Benedict's lifetime, the institutional and clerical Church was increasing in both power and authority, despite its being beset by internal doctrinal disputes and legal wrangling. For the first half of Benedict's life, there was something of a resurgence of Roman culture, a final flowering, under the tolerant stability of the Arian Ostrogothic king, Theodoric. For the rest of the sixth century, the rebuilding of Rome, in the form of churches and monasteries, was moving ahead through a combination of lay and clerical Christian power. St Benedict's monasteries were essentially communities of laymen (we know from the Rule of Benedict's reluctance to admit priests), and Richard Newman has seen them as "an attempt to conserve what was best in the old forms of lay piety and lay leadership, centered on the Roman household."[14] The monastic household was run on traditional lines, much like, we might imagine, Benedict's own home in Nursia. The abbot has all the concentrated authority of the Roman *paterfamilias*, who was also a *dominus—dominus et abbas* (RB 63:13), reflecting both Roman and scriptural traditions

14   Ibid., 76.

of authority. The learning of Benedict's monastery was also the private learning of the household (for self-improvement, especially at the spiritual level), certainly amateur, perhaps even haphazard, but fundamental to the good life that Benedict presents to those who might come to his community. St Benedict says that the monastery is to be constituted as *dominici schola servitii*, a "school for the Lord's service," and this phrase is not only at the heart of monastic life, but also of Benedictine education.

The Latin *schola* means a place of leisure, and in this sense it connects with the Latin distinction between *otium* (leisure) and *negotium* (not leisure, or work). Benedict well knows that human beings cannot work all the time, even if *ora et labora* (pray and work) does in a way sum up the life of the monastery. Chapter 48 of the Rule says at least as much about reading as it does about manual work, its ostensible subject; this suggests the underlying theme is really that of balance between *otium* and *negotium*, and a sense that both are part of the same thing: the spiritual activity that lies in the activity of heart, mind and body, to counter the *otiositas* (leisure, idleness) that is the enemy of the soul. In being highly prescriptive about the need to spend leisure time in reading, Benedict is maintaining the higher sense of the right use of *otium* that was central to the Roman idea of *humanitas*.[15] The Benedictine monastery enables the existence of people who are devoted to both work and the leisure that alone can foster the existence of a higher culture. While it is undoubtedly true that, as David Knowles says, "the monks for whom the Rule was written were not students," and that "St Benedict's reading was reading done for the benefit of the monk's own soul,"[16] it is also true that in the centuries immediately following Benedict, and especially in those centuries called by historians "the Benedictine Centuries"

---

15   Cf. Jean Leclercq, *The Love of Learning and the Desire for God: A Study of Monastic Culture* (New York, NY: Fordham University Press, 1982), 67: "*Otium* lies midway between the two perils *otiositas* and *negotium*, which is the very denial of *otium*. *Otium* is the major occupation of the monk. It is a very busy leisure, *negotisissimum otium*, as St Bernard and so many others have repeated."

16   David Knowles, *The Benedictines* (Eugene, OR: Wipf and Stock, 2009), 4.

(AD 900-1200), the Benedictines would become the first school-
masters of the emerging Christendom. But the employment of
monks to fill so many of the positions in Church and state where
learning was required happened because there was no one else,
rather than because monks were deliberately trained in the skills
and qualities that society needed: this was not the case. St Benedict's prescription of reading is as far from instrumentality as can
be imagined: it is a thing *per se* rather than *per usum*. But in doing
something for its own sake — to meet the needs of the higher
reaches of human nature — a consequence is a utility for others.

The right use of leisure, then, seems to be at the heart of the
meaning of Benedictine learning. Benedict prescribes no curriculum, although a sensible reading of Gregory's *Life* is that Benedict
himself, however "unschooled," was not unlearned. Rather, he saw
the wider context — practical, quotidian, integrated — in which
learning must subsist in the spiritual life, that is, the life of the
human being fully alive. Reading exists for the monk within the
larger pattern of work and prayer, and Benedictine education, from
the earliest times, has always had this implication: the deepest
learning will have the most profound effects for the individual
learner and for his society. Benedictine learning is the opposite of
what Benedict himself likely tired of in Rome: an education not
for the moral life, the *humanitas* of Cicero (following the *paideia*
and *arête* of the Greeks) but — where any education at all could be
found in a Roman society increasingly vitiated of talent, skill, and
wisdom — a facile and sophistical cleverness, a self-congratulatory
mental agility, a habit of superficial worldly success, suitable to
the politics of the time. In the education of Benedict's Rome there
was, historians generally agree, an "absence of any informing ideal
of moral excellence.... It needed a faith with emotive and revolu-
tionary appeal, capable of undermining indifference, of exposing
superficiality, of giving direction."[17] Until such time as European
education in the widest sense could be thoroughly animated with
the Christian faith, coming to fill the vacuum left by the old Roman

---

17   E. B. Castle, *Ancient Education and Today* (London: Penguin, 1964), 152.

world now receding from view, a learning based in true wisdom would be fostered in the reading, teaching, and learning of the monasteries. If there is to be for us, as Alasdair MacIntyre suggests we need, a new St Benedict, however different he might be from the first Benedict, he will know that only a deep learning — that is, integrated with the depths of the human mind and heart — will be of any lasting significance for human nature and society.

BENEDICTINE HISTORY

The long history of the Benedictines includes many beginnings and foundations, many reforms and revivals. Monte Cassino, as we have seen, continues to this day. Like a self-regenerating organism, Benedictine life returns after it is cut down. Unlike more recently founded orders of religious life (for example the Dominicans and the Franciscans of the High Middle Ages, and the Jesuits of the modern period), the Benedictine order, in Cardinal Newman's words, "is an organization, diverse, complex, and irregular, and variously ramified, rich rather than symmetrical, with many origins and centers and new beginnings and the action of local influences, like some great natural growth; with tokens, on the face of it, of its being a divine work, not the mere creation of human genius."[18] Despite the vicissitudes of its history, and the times and places wherein monasticism seems to have been extinguished, it can be argued with some force that no other institution, movement, or organization has had such a decisive effect on the character of Western Christian civilization, contributing in a major way, too, to its spread into the Americas, Africa, Asia, and Australasia. Writing in the middle of the nineteenth century, Newman said: "The panegyrists of this illustrious Order are accustomed to claim for it in all its branches as many as 37,000 houses, and, besides, 30 Popes, 200 Cardinals, 4 Emperors, 46 Kings, 51 Queens, 1,406 Princes, 1,600 Archbishops, 600 Bishops, 2,400 Nobles, and 15,000

18   John Henry Newman, "The Mission of St Benedict" (1859). http://www.newmanreader.org/works/historical/volume2/benedictine/schools.html.

Abbots and learned men."[19] And yet all this was the result of a
"slow-burn." There is no Benedictine "scheme" beyond the sense
that we live and work only *now*, in the present moment, in which
we should however be as fully aware as we can of the eternal. Both
past and future can be left to God.

In modernity, this can make Benedictine life and education
seem unhelpful. Something more energetic, deliberate, and consciously progressive is to be desired, something that focuses on
man and his immediate needs. Both Reformation and Revolution
threatened to sweep away monasticism as an obscurantist relic of
the past, and yet there was a resurgence in the nineteenth century, with new movements and congregations arising not only in
Europe but in North and South America, and monasteries founded
all over the world. In 1893, Pope Leo XIII was moved to establish
the office of Abbot Primate, resident in the college of Sant'Anselmo
on the Aventine in Rome, so important did he feel it was that the
Benedictines, for all the deeply cherished independence of their
houses, be established under one head at the heart of the Church.
Time and again it seems that modernity does not have the answers
to its own problems; cut off from the past, it keeps returning to
it as the only possible alternative to its own rootlessness. Mean-
while, the Benedictines, like the bees in Virgil, go about their daily
business of bringing the future into being. In a time when the
machine-world of industrial production seems ever expanding,
those things which are other to it — nature, beauty, the human
heart — need to find a language, a way of life, to survive and grow.
In the modern world of measurements, success is defined in physical terms, by that which is faster, bigger, taller — the celebration
of power. The destruction of Monte Cassino in 1944 seems such
a defining moment in a war described by Evelyn Waugh as "the
modern age in arms."[20] Yet Monte Cassino was (again) rebuilt,
and monastic life is there continued. This is the lasting theme of
Benedictine history, not death but rebirth.

19   Ibid.
20   Evelyn Waugh, *Men at Arms* (London: Penguin, 1964), 12.

Throughout their history, the Benedictines have educated the young, as well as the old, in the things of permanent value, as reflected in the scriptures, the Church Fathers, and the humane letters of the Roman inheritance. We know from the Rule that boys were educated in monasteries, and that schools were coterminous with monastic foundations. We have seen that the oldest continually existing school in the world seems to be what is now known as The King's School (since its re-foundation at the Dissolution by Henry VIII), in Canterbury, England, the school having existed since the foundation there of a Benedictine community by St Augustine in 597: here is another enduring symbol of Benedictine education. While it is true that episcopal as well as monastic schools have existed since late antiquity, it is also true that many of the cathedral schools were also monastic; in England, for example, half the cathedrals had Benedictine priories attached to them. Non-episcopal sites in England were also usually Benedictine, for instance Westminster Abbey. Benedictine education is thus a long and resilient thread connecting the modern world with late antiquity. From its roots in that soil, it continues to find sustenance in the pre-modern world, and in this sense it predates not only industrialism but also the Enlightenment, the Reformation, the Renaissance, and the Medieval culture it largely created.

It is convenient to see the birth of that Medieval culture in the Carolingian Renaissance in the eighth century, yet it was in the northeastern isles off mainland Europe that the Dark Ages were to become luminescent, first in Ireland in the fifth century, and then in England in the sixth. It was here that St Bede the Venerable in Northumbria, and later Alcuin in York — both monks of the Benedictine Rule — became the greatest of the early medieval teachers and writers. In 781, Alcuin came to Charlemagne's court at Aachen to help make a new kind of "academy," as he put it. Under Charlemagne, too, the Rule of St Benedict became, through the standardizing reforms of St Benedict of Aniane, the preeminent monastic rule in the Frankish empire, a situation that continued even after the fall of the Carolingians. Charlemagne's son Louis the Pious had received a monastic education; he not only formalized the instruction that all monasteries in the empire were to follow the Benedictine Rule, but he also adopted the Rule as the basis for his government of the Empire — perhaps the first time that the Rule was used thus as a model for leadership outside the monastery. Thus was Benedictine influence on the whole culture of Europe established. The Carolingian Renaissance was itself the result of a movement to reorder the liturgy and monastic life, and a literary revival, based on the study of grammar as St Benedict prescribes, was also a consequence. As Jean Leclercq put it: "Such is the true character of the culture which had paved the way for the Carolingian reform: a humanism wholly inspired by classical antiquity, a humanism whose touchstone is Christ crucified, risen from the dead, who by His example and His grace makes us renounce evil in order to lead us to the heavenly city."[21] Benedictine life shows that grammar can — in no insignificant sense — lead to God.[22]

Benedictine learning, in all its breadth and inclusiveness, leads back to this higher (or deeper) purpose: compunction of heart, the turning of the soul towards God. This is not an easy idea for the modern world to understand or value. In modernity, words such as *God* and *soul* are highly problematic, and modern man is pre-occupied with, even if bewildered by, himself and his immediate challenges, and his scheme of self-perfection. The traditionally (and truly) human and those things that constitute it become destabilized in the modern world, afflicted by all sorts of discontinuities. The connections of man to his family, his past, his own life of work, commitments and relationships, the natural and the built environment, the transcendent values of beauty, truth, and goodness: all these aspects of the human are now fraught with doubt, which makes us experience something akin to decline and decay. The world must be renewed, since it is a place of death, as well as of life. The history of the Benedictines suggests that the

---

21   Leclercq, 40.
22   Cf. ibid., 53: "The content of monastic culture has seemed to be symbolized, synthesized in these two words: grammar and spirituality."

way of Benedict has something to say to all people, in all places and at all times in their need:

> This may be taken to illustrate St. Benedict's mode of counteracting the miseries of life. He found the world, physical and social, in ruins, and his mission was to restore it in the way, not of science, but of nature, not as if setting about to do it, not professing to do it by any set time or by any rare specific or by any series of strokes, but so patiently, gradually, that often, till the work was done, it was not known to be doing. It was a restoration, rather than a visitation, correction or conversion. The new world which he helped to create was a growth rather than a structure.[23]

The cultivation of human beings, like that of a garden or a countryside, takes many such small actions carried out in an abiding faith and spirit.

BENEDICTINE EDUCATION TODAY

A suitable starting point for any consideration of education, and a question that any teacher should ask of their prospective students, is: "Who is there with a love of true life and a longing for days of real fulfillment?" (*RB*: Prologue, 15). This is the challenge that St Benedict poses to those who come to consider life in the monastery, the pattern of which he lays down in his Rule. For centuries, this has also been the promise of Benedictine education. The monastery itself is, as Benedict puts it, "a school of the Lord's service," and for most of the nearly 1,500 years since Benedict of Nursia wrote his Rule for monks, his monasteries have provided an education for the young, making Benedictine schools the very oldest continuous form of Catholic education. The present-day Benedictine schools from around the world, part

23   John Henry Newman, "The Mission of St Benedict."

of the Benedictine Educators Network (BeNet), are currently exploring in a spirit of *ressourcement* and mutual support the nature of what they are called to do now for the Church and the world. It is an international Benedictine project considering how to provide the young with the spiritual, intellectual, and emotional nurturing they need to experience "a love of true life, and days of real fulfillment."

Benedictine learning provided a cradle of education for the Church and early Christendom, informing all aspects of its subsequent development. In "The Mission of St Benedict," Newman discerns three historical phases in Christian education, corresponding to the three periods — ancient, medieval and modern — of Church and world history. Each period is characterized by one of the great Orders: the ancient by the Benedictines, the medieval by the Dominicans, and the modern by the Jesuits. The spirit of the learning of each era is reflected in, and partly formed by, the spirit of the Order: the ancient by the poetic vision, the medieval by the rational, and the modern by the prudential. Thus, in Newman's analysis, St Benedict stands for the Imagination, St Dominic for Science, and St Ignatius for Practical Sense. Newman's picture of the Benedictine *charism*, as involving a particular form of spiritual insight, is helpful in showing what Benedictine education offers the world today.

The heritage of 1,500 years of Benedictine culture (far more than wines, honey, and Gregorian chant, however well these artifacts symbolize "a true life, and days of real fulfillment") is our common heritage: not for nothing is St Benedict known as the Patriarch of the West, and Patron of Europe. When Cardinal Ratzinger chose Benedict as his papal name, it was with a conscious sense of what St Benedict has to say to us today. Benedict of Nursia wrote his Rule very much aware of living in times of decline. We are also aware today of living in times when the order of Europe is disturbed, amid profound change and upheaval. The young, especially, are aware of instability — in family life, in the world of work and business, and in a sense of isolation and fear for the future; they are keenly aware, too, of right and wrong, the use and abuse of the environment, and the immense possibilities, for good or ill, of digital technology. What can young people expect to experience in the coming century? It may be a time when imagination is needed, more than reason or even prudence, however much these faculties will never be superfluous. The Benedictine commitment to listening (obedience), *conversatio morum* (the spiritual transformation of life), and *stabilitas loci* (making a home, brightening the corner in which one finds oneself, and sanctifying the everyday) presents a valuable way of responding to the challenges of the world, capable of providing both individuals and communities with a life worth living, in time and for eternity. The Benedictine gift for bringing the secular order under cultivation, under the tool of *ora et labora*, the hard-edged ploughshare of the monastic discipline, enables the planting of the Gospel in the human heart, to bear fruit in civility, learning, beauty, and peace. This is what once made the civilization of Europe, and may help today in its recovery.

The American and Canadian Association of Benedictine Colleges and Universities has identified ten hallmarks of a Benedictine educational institution: love, prayer, stability, *conversatio morum*, obedience, discipline, humility, stewardship, hospitality, and community. Of all these valuable things, St Benedict had most to say about humility, which for him is first among the virtues, and makes all the others possible. Humility is the receptive condition in which we recognize our humanity, in all its possibilities and weaknesses. Humility shows us our groundedness in earth, paradoxically our surest start on the way to heaven, inviting gratitude as the proper response to the given. The more a Benedictine educational institution is true to itself and its vocation, the more it engages in a particular kind of learning, one which characterized the beginnings of the medieval world in the ancient one, when monastic culture was pervasive, before the scholasticism of the friars and the universities, and before the great Ignatian project of a practical Catholic education in the modern period. St Benedict emphasizes the heart more than the head, and as our culture more and more turns away from the Enlightenment privileging of reason, so the value of *sapientia* rather than of *scientia* might once again come to the fore. Our culture has a choice: one alternative to modern reason is madness, but another is the wisdom of God.

Monastic learning in the ancient and early medieval world was grounded in the practice of *lectio divina*, the attentive, prayerful reading of Scripture. This was at the heart of the development of the literary culture that spread learning into the medieval period and thence into modernity. After the dominance of scholasticism and neo-scholasticism, in which the practice of *lectio divina* declined, there was renewal of interest in the middle of the last century, and it was re-emphasized in Vatican II. *Lectio* has become a major tool of good works in the hands of the South American lay Benedictine Manquehue Apostolic Movement. *Lectio* used in the context of *tutoría*, or spiritual friendship among the young, allows Chilean visitors to the English Benedictine schools to establish self-running *lectio divina* groups among English teenagers. It was a powerful thing when a young Benedictine pupil, in one of the schools, led a *lectio* session in a group comprised of several headmasters and a Cardinal: here, perhaps, is a sign for the future of the Church. And the fourfold structure of *lectio divina* — reading, meditation, prayer, and contemplation — can also become a way of transforming what happens in the classroom to build a new, authentic Catholic curriculum, reintroducing a culture of deep reading in an educational world where reading has become the skimming of screens for *information*. Rather, *lectio* is about reading for the *formation* of students, preparatory to the *transformation* of persons and society. As Pope Benedict XVI said in 2005, "If [*lectio divina*] is effectively promoted, this practice will bring to the Church — I am convinced of it — a new spiritual springtime."[24]

Benedictine culture, like the form of Catholic education that arises out of it, is seen in *a quality of making*. Benedictine artifacts — whether a homily, a liturgy, a book of hours, a church, a

24   Benedict XVI, Address to the Participants in the International Congress Organized to Commemorate the 40th Anniversary of the Dogmatic Constitution on Divine Revelation *Dei Verbum* (Castel Gandolfo, September 16, 2005), http://w2.vatican.va/content/benedict-xvi/en/speeches/2005/september/documents/hf_ben-xvi_spe_20050916_40-dei-verbum.html.

treatise, a piece of sacred art or music — are characterized by an intensity of focus, a luminous order, a precision of craftsmanship, and a lack of redundancy, wherein the form agrees well with the function. Benedictine artifacts reflect the desire that God be glorified in all things, and they are paradigms of the harmonious integration of matter and spirit, implying everywhere a *both-and* rather than an *either-or* mental construction. Benedictine communities (including almost the only Catholic schools now where the full ecclesial community — priests, religious, and laity — works and lives together) provide a model of living that sustains heart, mind, and body, and cultivates the integrated personality, a spiritual ecology suggested in the *viriditas* ("greenness") of Benedictines such as St Gregory the Great and St Hildegard of Bingen. The wisdom of the pre-scientific world, in which learning is pursued not for instrumental ends of getting and spending but for living better lives, provides a powerful inspiration for the future of Catholic education, and education everywhere.

CHAPTER 2

Spirit

THE RULE

The Rule of St Benedict is a relatively short work of some 12,000 words, just over half of which are quotations from scripture or liturgical directions. Since the 1930's it has gradually become clear to scholars that it is not entirely original but rather has an especial debt to an earlier text known as the Rule of the Master. However, just as a Shakespeare play is usually indebted to some earlier version of the story, the genius of Benedict's Rule lies in the changes he has made to his sources.[1] The moderation and discretion of the Rule are what mark it out from the harsher monastic rules that originated in the essentially eremitic monastic life of Egypt, or the Celtic monasticism of Ireland. The Rule has also been prized for its realism, practicality, and common-sense approach. Benedict's Rule is more suited both to his particular aims in his conception of monastic life, especially in community, and to the nature of life in the western and northern countries of Europe. Benedict describes his text as a "little Rule for beginners," and despite the later identification of the regular life — that is, lived according to a Rule — with clericalism and the priesthood, it is essentially written for laymen living a religious life in community. Apart from its intrinsic qualities, it also owes its later ascendancy in Western monasticism to two figures surnamed "the Great": one a pope, St Gregory I, and the other an emperor, Charles I, whom we know as Charlemagne.[2]

As we have seen, Benedict's Rule is thoroughly Roman in spirit, and this made it attractive to the Romanizing spirit of the

---

1 Cf. Knowles, *The Benedictines*, 9.
2 Cf. Joseph H. Lynch, *The Medieval Church: A Brief History* (London: Longman, 1992), 79.

Carolingian project. David Knowles judged that St Benedict, one of the last of the Romans, was "more truly Roman in spirit than even Gregory the Great":

> The impression of sanity, of strength, of moderation and of stability — typical qualities of the noblest Romans — is not merely subjective; it is noteworthy that in such a short document as the Rule the word *gravitas* (dignity) occurs five times, *rationabilis* (reasonable) and its adverb five times, *imperium* (authority) six times, *stabilis* and *stabilitas* (steadfast) six times and *mensura* and *mensurate* (measure, moderation) ten times. This sense of strong government, of stability and yet of moderation, was precisely the quality most needed in one who was to hand down the wisdom of the desert to a new, adolescent, uncultivated age of shifting landmarks and peoples.[3]

It is also noteworthy that Benedict made the times of prayer in the Rule coincide with the changing of the Roman imperial guard.[4] Benedict was likely writing the Rule later in his life at Monte Cassino, when Italy was returning, after the death of Theodoric, to war and consequent social upheaval. There is an intriguing theory, advanced by Abbot John Chapman, that Benedict wrote the Rule (at the invitation of Pope Hormisdas) to standardize monastic practice, and whether this theory is true or not, the Rule does manage to distill the best of various monastic traditions.

The Rule of St Benedict is distinctive in being much more oriented towards community living than previous rules, which were more redolent of the origins of monasticism in the life of hermits (the prefix *mon-* in *monasticism* or *monachism* being a clue to the fact). There is a new emphasis on altruism (cf. *RB* 72), the

3   David Knowles, *Saints and Scholars: Twenty-Five Medieval Portraits* (Cambridge: Cambridge University Press, 1962), 6.

4   See Stephen Thomas Berg, "St Benedict's Enduring Rule." http://www.growmercy.org/wp-content/uploads/St.%20Benedict%27s%20Enduring%20Rule.pdf.

need to focus on what is better for others, not what is better for oneself. The modern reader coming fresh to the Rule, however, will note the extent of the abbot's authority, and that essentially his authority is final under God (not forgetting popes, and the need to accommodate local bishops in some respects). Christian thinking in the fifth century was increasingly emphasizing the role of leaders as stewards, God being the ultimate and only real *dominus*, and this too is evident in the large part of the Rule that deals with the abbot. But the bottom line in the Rule is that the monk owes his abbot complete obedience, a completeness with origins in the complete authority of Roman fathers over their children. Even the balancing of the authority of the abbot with the taking of counsel from the community is based on the Roman family *consilium*, which the *paterfamilias* was not obliged to follow.[5] In Benedict's Rule, however, the abbot is much more integrated with the Rule itself, which is over him as well as over the other monks. St Benedict's Rule also emphasizes in a new way — and a way that was to help create social coherence in the new Europe that emerged in the early Middle Ages — the importance of *stabilitas loci*, the monk staying in, or a part of, the community of his profession. St Benedict is especially scathing about the custom of monks wandering from monastery to monastery. The wholeness of spirit in the Rule is one of its most distinguishing features. St Benedict himself is depersonalized, seen only in his work, which is profoundly affirming of the human. The Rule displays "a spirit of trust in human nature aided by grace; the utterance of a man who, after long and often bitter experience of human weakness and malice still firmly believed that men could become true sons of God and in so doing could help others to go with them."[6]

What are the implications of and value in the Rule for the business of education? We have seen, thus far, that the Rule places a very firm emphasis on the need for reading. While St Benedict has sometimes been read, or misread, as anti-intellectual, and although

5 Richard Newman, 66.
6 Knowles, *Saints and Scholars*, 11.

he does not say a great deal about just what must be read (perhaps because he takes much for granted about it and, characteristically, avoids micro-management of things that can be left to themselves), "St Benedict's legislation on reading has not always secured the attention it deserves. Its full implications can only be grasped by those who follow with some care a reconstruction of the daily life in St Benedict's monastery and discover that little less than four hours were daily devoted to reading, as compared to some six given to work."[7] The practice of daily reading is the mustard seed from which the great tree of Benedictine learning grows. Benedict makes senior monks patrol the monastery to see that the prescribed reading periods are being observed, and a stylus and writing tablet were part of every monk's basic equipment.[8] Much reading is evidenced by Benedict himself in the Rule: "One finds Benedict quoting St Augustine, St Jerome, St Cyprian and St Leo while also displaying a conversance with St Basil, St Pachomius, St Macarius of Alexandria, St Orsiesius and other anonymous rules. Notably, his training in pagan classics, such as Virgil and Sallust, can also be traced."[9] The combination of Christian and pre-Christian literature in the Rule sets the template for the subsequent spirit of Benedictine education, and apart from anything else illustrates that it encompasses material of both divine and human value. Reading is the gateway to formation for human freedom. As Raymond Studzinski has put it, "Reading, meditating, and praying centered on the Word of God gradually inscribed that Word in fleshly existence and transformed the monastic into a self that, like an illuminated manuscript, rendered the sacred text in a colorful, artistic way for others to 'read.'"[10]

Another benefit of an education with the Rule of St Benedict at its heart is the spiritual context it provides for reading in a way antithetical to an instrumental approach to study. Nowadays

7   Ibid., 13–14.
8   Richard Newman, 34.
9   Berg.
10   Raymond Studzinski, *Reading to Live: The Evolving Practice of Lectio Divina* (Collegeville, MN: Liturgical Press, 2009), 126.

the advantages bestowed by education are usually taken to be economic, either for individuals or for society. The pursuit of knowledge for its own end, as in Newman's defense of a liberal education, or the pursuit of wisdom in a more specifically spiritual and Benedictine sense, on the face of it does not address seriously enough the need to acquire the very best academic qualifications for proceeding to the next level of education, or to successful employment and economic well-being. Yet the key to understanding the place of studies in Benedictine education is that they are not really an end in themselves, but point to a higher kind of utility, such that studies are not entirely disconnected from manual work. The effect of Benedict's Rule was to create within the context of monastic living a radically new approach to manual work— the servile arts — more in keeping with the spirit of Rome, perhaps, than of Athens. Artisans are specifically addressed in the Rule, showing that the economic viability of monastic life was always a consideration. The Cistercian reform of the Rule was partly to re-emphasize the importance of manual work, and the extension of monastic life, through the lay-brothers, to those who were not literate. Benedictine learning, therefore, does not over-privilege the idea of a liberal education, although it can certainly include it. The effects of reading may take many forms in the Benedictine tradition, not just scholarship.

The principle of freedom runs through the Benedictine tradition, and this is deeply connected with the emphasis on reading. Cardinal Newman was devoted to the Athenian spirit of personal, internalized human freedom, and he liked to see this in a religious form in the Oratorians, the congregation he joined. He would allude to Pericles' famous funeral oration, where the orator contrasts the spirit of Athens with that of Sparta; the contrast is between an inner freedom of choice and a system of external discipline. Newman saw the Jesuit system as being like Sparta, so where might we place the Benedictines? On the principle of balance, between the two extremes of the individualistic but collegial spirit of the Oratorians and the corporate military discipline that inspires the Jesuits, the Benedictines are in the middle. The communal spirit is stronger than in either the Oratorians or the Jesuits, neither of whom have the requirement to sing the Office together in choir (the Oratorians are not, in fact, regulars). All three orders have their own kind of freedom, either pastoral or intellectual, but the work of Benedictines (including the Cistercians) is quite unpredictable, incorporating at one end the agricultural, the architectural, and the industrial, through arts and crafts, to the scientific, the philosophical, and the theological at the other. The contemplation of nature and the imaginative recreation of the monk in his work might take any form so long as his community and his abbot approve of his pursuit. This is a valuable example to us today in thinking about where education in a Benedictine setting might lead its pupils, and their future work. Whether obviously possessing utility or not, if it is filled with the Benedictine spirit it will be of benefit to the individual and the community and will, at some level, glorify God.

LECTIO DIVINA

After the Rule itself, the Benedictine spirit (especially insofar as it affects education) seems best exemplified, preserved, and passed on in the practice of *lectio divina*, or spiritual reading. On the first level, Benedict of course wishes for the monks to devote themselves to the reading of the scriptures and Patristic (for instance) commentaries. Benedict would have understood the concept of reading, and even that of *lectio divina*, differently than we do. Reading, for the early Benedictines, meant an activity that integrated body and mind: "when *legere* and *lectio* are used without further explanation, they mean an activity which, like chant and writing, requires the participation of the whole body and the whole mind. Doctors of ancient times used to recommend reading to their patients as a physical exercise on an equal level with walking, running, or ball-playing."[11] We should note also the close connection, from the earliest times in Benedictine history, of writing and

11   Leclercq, 15.

singing with reading. It is constantly seen in Benedictine life that one thing is connected to one or more other things, just as are people in a community. *Lectio* itself is connected to other activities, in a way delineated after Benedict (notably by Guigo II the Carthusian), as a fourfold process of *lectio, meditatio, oratio,* and *contemplatio.* The stages of reading, meditating, praying, and contemplating can be seen as a microcosm of all Benedictine life and learning, the end of which is not so much intellectual progress but spiritual growth, aiming not so much for *truth* as for *heaven* — bearing in mind of course that these two things are not antithetical, rather that the latter is the spiritual "place" of the former.

The early Christian Fathers such as Jerome and Augustine were at pains to make a separation in practice between Christian learning and the pagan culture that prevailed at the time. On the other hand, both Jerome and Augustine also praise the pagan authors, particularly where they happen to conform to Christian standards. What is beyond argument is that medieval learning involved an increasingly wide and deep acquaintance with the classics, and divergent opinions about them. It is sometimes suggested, however, that because the Rule of St Benedict says nothing of a *scriptorium* or of a curriculum, Benedict must not have valued reading beyond the scriptures and Fathers. A contrast between Benedict and Cassiodorus as monastic founders is sometimes drawn. Cassiodorus was a Roman statesman who founded a monastery at Vivarium and wrote a program of studies for the monks called the *Institutiones,* the basis for the later medieval understanding of the seven liberal arts, the *trivium* and the *quadrivium.* Cassiodorus quotes Cicero alongside scripture, and he established at Vivarium an emphasis on the copying of texts; his monastery-school links the spiritual life with study. St Benedict, on the other hand, never mentions study in the same way; his view is of *one* thing rather than *two.* But the history of the Benedictine order is the fruit of the freedom of the Rule, a little rule for beginners, as Benedict puts it. Programs of study can become dated, and the Rule of St Benedict addresses first principles. By saying no more about reading and study than that they must take place for about four hours on a daily basis, Benedict establishes a characteristic feature of the Rule with regard to learning: that it can and should take many forms and include many things. One of those things would certainly be humane letters.

The practice of *lectio* — of reading — is at the heart of the transformative power of Benedictine living and learning. Rather as the copying, internalizing, and transmission of both Christian and pagan texts would transform the culture and civilization of Europe during the Middle Ages, so the process of reading, writing about, and discussing texts has a transformative effect on individual persons. The value of *lectio* for Benedictine education today is primarily evangelical:

> *Lectio divina*, especially when done with the Scriptures, enjoys in this twenty-first century a place of prominence among practices of Christian spirituality across denominational lines. Because of its transformative power it deserves such recognition. As a result of the practice of *lectio* people find themselves feeling, imagining, thinking, and acting differently. They acquire the "mind of Christ" and are readied to transform the world as Christ did. The power of the practice to change people is amazing.[12]

But as Raymond Studzinski implies in the above, the effects are not caused simply by the scriptures but by the process of reading itself: "All reading holds out the possibility of conversion."[13] Reading takes us out of ourselves, into a new place, and this sense of the text as a place connects reading with the Benedictine vow of stability: "As Burrows comments: 'The reader, bound to the monastery as to a single dwelling place in order to fulfill the vow of *stabilitas loci*, comes to the text with a similar commitment: he makes a life-long choice to stay in one "place" and this means that

---

12   Studzinski, 200. On the powerful effect of *lectio divina* on the lives of prisoners, see Alexander McLean, "A Prisoner by Choice: Discovering God's Word in Prison," *Identity* 45 (2018): 10–11.

13   Ibid., 201.

he will "live" in one text until death.'"[14] This textual "place" is of course the scriptures, but in entering any textual place the reader is taken out of the self in a way that is also a confrontation with the self in a truly educative process.

If we grant that St Benedict built a certain amount of freedom into his conception of reading and studies, then it follows that Benedictine reading is an encounter with human freedom. Beyond the canon of scripture itself, Benedict is not prescriptive: there is no literary canon that must be studied, in contrast to the project of Cassiodorus, or the *ratio studiorum* of the Jesuits. This is not to imply a relativism of reading, as is often implied in some forms of education, that anything can be read with profit and the analytical skill that goes with reading can be applied to any material: this seems to set up a false, an unreal, distinction. The material given for reading, suggests the Rule of St Benedict, must be such as to promote spiritual growth rather than be the object of intellectual curiosity. But that which can promote spiritual growth might include much of both divine and human origin, and here the Benedictine spirit is inclusive, so that the preservation of the most valuable of pre-Christian literature was an unavoidable consequence of Benedictine monastic culture. This is also a consequence of Benedict's sympathetic understanding of human nature; as much as the Renaissance humanists, he shows that a correct understanding of human nature is essential if the sowing of the Gospel seed is to be successful. It is this realism that must subsist in any education of permanent value. Both teachers and students need to see things — including themselves — as they really are if conversion of life is to begin, continue, and become a constant vocational disposition. This disposition involves, through the reading of a text, an understanding of self through *story*.

Here we come to a problem: modern man is unsure of his place in the story. The cultural critic George Steiner has spoken of "an unhousedness, of our eviction from a central humanity in the face of the tidal provocations of political barbarism and technocratic

14 Ibid., 153.

servitude, if we do not redefine, if we do not re-experience, the life
of meaning in the text, in music, in art. We must come to recognize, and the stress is on *re*-cognition, a meaningfulness which is
that of a freedom of giving and reception beyond the constraints
of immanence."[15] But in our modern homelessness, new narratives — ultimately unsatisfying to the human spirit — intrude:
"therapeutic (everything can be treated), technological (everything
can be fixed), consumerist (what one wants, one can get), and
militaristic (forces fighting against the therapeutic, technological,
and consumerist scripts can be thwarted)."[16] *Lectio divina* involves
the cultivation of grammar, the art of reading, which is the active
process of interacting with the world, so as to read things as they
are, and to see our place in the story. In the widest as well as the
nearest sense, Benedictine *lectio* is the beginning of the encounter
with the Gospel, the completed story at the heart of the universe,[17]
written in the language of the Logos, and which can be read in
the sacred Name of God, YHWH, "I am that I am."[18]

BENEDICTINE POETRY

The third aspect of the Benedictine spirit might be described as
the response to reading, or the activity that comes out of reading
or *lectio*, and which St John Henry Newman described as *poetry*.
Monastic life was "a return to that primitive age of the world,
of which poets have so often sung, the simple life of Arcadia or
the reign of Saturn, when fraud and violence were unknown."[19]

15   George Steiner, *Real Presences* (Chicago, IL: University of Chicago Press,
1991), 50.

16   Walter Brueggemann, "Counterscript," *Christian Century*, 122 (November
29, 2005): 22–23. Quoted in Studzinski, 209.

17   On the Gospel as the truest of true stories, see J. R. R. Tolkien, *On Fairy
Stories* (London: Harper Collins, 2008), 78.

18   The sacred Name of God, also referred to as the Tetragrammaton, translit-
erated from Hebrew as YHWH and often rendered as Yahweh, has been explained
as meaning "I am that I am," or "I am so that I am." It is thus in itself a complete
grammatical statement, and contains the whole story of the universe, into the
life of which we are taken up in Christ.

19   John Henry Newman, "The Mission of St Benedict."

Benedictine poetry, then, for Newman, is rooted in a way of life that goes back to beginnings, to fundamentals; in the way that human beings interact with each other, with nature, and with God. Newman goes on to say what he means by "poetry" in this context: "Poetry, then, I conceive, whatever be its metaphysical essence, or however various may be its kinds, whether it more properly belongs to action or to suffering, nay, whether it is more at home with society or with nature, whether its spirit is seen to best advantage in Homer or in Virgil, at any rate, is always the antagonist to *science*."[20] Newman's distinction makes clear sense in the context of his time, when the opposition (unknown in antiquity and very largely unknown in the medieval world) between art and science had already become quite marked: "Poetry does not address the reason, but the imagination and affections."[21] Newman also talks of the poetry of Benedictine life in its houses of old establishment and of country settings, sometimes misinterpreted "as chosen by a sort of sentimental, ornamental indolence."[22] Not so, says Newman; for the poetry of the medieval monks "was the poetry of hard work and hard fare, unselfish hearts and charitable hands."[23] The beautiful landscapes of modern Europe were often the result of the labors of monks and lay brothers in lands previously uncultivated.

And this is the clue to how we should understand Newman's reading of Benedictine "poetry," which is very much grounded in its root sense of *poiesis*. The distinction Newman makes between poetry and science is essentially one between a *sacramental* and an *analytical* disposition, between the mysticism of St Bernard (*credo ut experiar*) and the scholasticism of St Anselm (*credo ut intelligam*). *Poiesis* is making; man is in the image of God in being a maker of symbols through imitation of creation. The poetic instinct involves a sacramental view of reality, such that signs, symbols, and metaphors — ways of speaking of one thing in terms

20   Ibid.
21   Ibid.
22   Ibid.
23   Ibid.

of another — are never *only* representations. The things of man's art, just like the things of creation, enact the deeper reality to which they refer. A poetic view of the world is a sacramental view; a sacramental view is a mystical view. The artifacts of the monastery take on this sacramental character, and indeed all the things of use are to be treated with the respect due to the vessels of the altar (*RB* 31). Even people themselves — especially visitors to the monastery — are signs of someone greater, that is, Christ himself. The abbot is adjured to consider the monks as vessels (*RB* 64) and avoid breaking them by attacking the rust too vigorously. The famous motto *ut in omnibus glorificetur Deus* (that God may be glorified in all things) appears in the relatively mundane context of the fixing of prices of artisanal products, at slightly less than what non-monastic workshops would charge (*RB* 57). In Benedict's sacramental view of reality, all in creation, including those good things that man makes in imitation of God, are to be considered as signs of God's presence. The ultimate human artifact, made by God with man's cooperation, is a human life well lived.

The importance of recalling the sacramental vision in modernity has been beautifully stated by the poet and painter David Jones. Jones himself was a frequent guest of the Cistercians on Caldey Island, and in his essay "Art and Sacrament" (1955), Jones refers to *poeta* as man's "unique title": "So that it is here supposed that man is a creature whose end is extra-mundane and whose nature is to make things and that the things made are not only things of mundane requirement but are of necessity the signs of something other. Further, that an element of the gratuitous adheres to this making."[24] This "gratuitousness" of man's making is in the sense of God's gratuitous act of making the universe. Man's work is "sign-making" and "man is unavoidably a sacramentalist.... His works are sacramental in character."[25] This means a kind of real presence within works of art: "For the painter may

24 David Jones, *Epoch and Artist: Selected Writings* (London: Faber and Faber, 2008), 150.
25 Ibid., 155.

say to himself: 'This is not a representation of a mountain, it *is* "mountain" under the form of paint.' Indeed, unless he says this unconsciously or consciously he will not be a painter worth a candle."[26] Jones asks whether or not it is "the trend of our technocracy to increasingly put asunder what is joined together in man-the-artist."[27] If so, then late- or post-modern man is moving further away from the truth of the universe revealed by Christ. "As a postscript," Jones writes, "I venture to ask the reader to consider what Maurice de la Taille said was done on Maundy Thursday by Good Friday's Victim; I quote: 'He placed himself in the order of signs.'"[28] Jones affirms here that the Sacraments of the Church are not a free-floating arbitrary construct, but exist as part of a larger language of signs that is built into the nature of the world of human existence. We read these signs in the language of the Logos in whom all things are made.

David Jones explicates something here which is implicit in all aspects of Benedictine living and making. Although the arbitrariness of signs is a commonplace in postmodern thought — reinforcing a subjectivism of value and truth — the Christian sense that the order of signs preserves the sacred is crucial in connecting human beings to eternity; the alternative is for man to be locked in himself, speaking his own sign-language of private meaning. A typical feature of Benedictine making — be it art, music, song, artifacts and crafts, gardens and architecture, or agriculture and manuscript illumination — is this quality of luminous order. The making reveals rather than obscures the transcendent qualities of God, such that the making is like a window through which a greater reality is figured-forth. The sacramental sense is opposed to the scientific approach to the world; to return to Newman: "The aim of Science is to get a hold of things, to grasp them, to handle them, to comprehend them; that is (to use the familiar term), to *master* them, or to be superior to them. Its success lies in being able

---

26 Ibid., 170.
27 Ibid., 178.
28 Ibid., 179.

to draw a line around them, and to tell where each of them is to be found within that circumference, and how each lies relatively to all the rest."[29] Modernity is of course founded on this approach, which when taken to its extreme threatens the existence of the sacramental sense in persons and in the culture. The poetical sense, by contrast, is essentially sacramental: Poetry "demands, as its primary condition, that we should not put ourselves above the objects in which it resides, but at their feet; that we should feel them to be above and beyond us, that we should look up to them, and that, instead of fancying that we can comprehend them, we should take for granted that we are surrounded and comprehended by them ourselves."[30] We shall allude to Benedictine science later on, but it is secondary, both historically and conceptually, to the poetic life that Newman identifies; even then, Benedictine science does not lose hold of sacramentality. It will be readily seen, too, that the disposition Newman is describing above is that quality of which St Benedict speaks more than anything else in his Rule: *humility.* As has been said elsewhere, this is his name for *wisdom.*

In late modernity, no one can seriously posit a form of education, in Benedictine schools or elsewhere, which does not address science as a priority. If only to understand the world we now live in, both knowledge and technology (things today usually summed up in the word science) must be part of the curriculum in any form of education that will support the young person's growth in the world today. And as we shall see, the Benedictines have never despised the technical. But unless our education is founded in the sacramental sense of the created world, we shall not enable persons or the culture to see things as they really are. This, too, is humility, and it will affect the way persons and communities, cities and countries interact with each other and with the natural and built environments. Nothing could be more relevant to education for today's world. It affects both man's making and his doing, both *poiesis* and *praxis*; and it necessitates a God- or Christ-centered

---

29 John Henry Newman, "The Mission of St Benedict."
30 Ibid.

approach to learning, because without the sacramental sense of the indwelling, the inhering of the Holy Spirit of God in all things that are good, then only a cold instrumentality, a sense of the deadness of all things, can logically follow. George Steiner has identified this problem of a modern culture that fails to see real presences:

> All good art and literature begin in immanence. But they do not stop there. Which is to say, very plainly, that it is the enterprise and privilege of the aesthetic to quicken into lit presence the continuum between temporality and eternity, between matter and spirit, between man and "the other." It is in this common and exact sense that *poiesis* opens on to, is underwritten by, the religious and the metaphysical. The questions: "What is poetry, music, art?" "How can they not be?" and "How do they act upon us and how do we interpret this action?" are, ultimately, theological questions.[31]

What Steiner implies is that a culture that turns its back on the religious and the theological will forget how to read the language of signs in which the world is written. Such a culture would be, as Steiner puts it, a culture of the *epilogue*, the after-word. It would have lost the power of language, the grammar (literature) that leads to God.

BENEDICTINE LIVES

What follows are sketches of five educators, four Benedictines and a Cistercian, who lived out, and taught within, the Rule of St Benedict. They are all members of a select group of thirty-six men and women whom the Catholic Church has formally recognized with the title of "Doctor of the Church," "Doctor" in this case meaning of course "teacher." They all embody, too, the characteristically

31 Steiner, 227.

Benedictine integration of the *vita contemplativa* and the *vita activa*, and they all display a rich range of human talents. As such they, along with many others who embody the spirit of Benedictine teaching and learning, can serve as examples for Benedictine educators today.

Pope St Gregory the Great (c. 540–604)

Gregory was born into an aristocratic Roman family and occupied high office in the Roman magistracy before founding, and entering, a monastery on the Caelian Hill in Rome. He was the abbot until he was made pope in 590.

Although there is no reason to think that he was actually a "Benedictine," living by Benedict's Rule, Gregory was the first monk to become pope, and he was one of the most important figures in the transition from late antiquity to the Middle Ages. The dominance of Western plainchant is attributed to him, but in addition to liturgical reform he was a considerable ecclesiastical administrator, sent Augustine to convert the Anglo-Saxons, was a mystic, theologian, and almsgiver. His book on church leadership, usually known as *Pastoral Care* (the *liber regulae pastoralis*), had immense influence well into the Middle Ages, and it was translated into English and promoted by King Alfred the Great.

Gregory typifies in the highest degree many facets of subsequent Benedictinism. He was pulled from the cloister to work at a high level in the world, but always remained at heart a monk. Gregory embodies both the contemplative and the active life, in a way that was to return a thousand years later, on the cusp of modernity, in St Thomas More: a man who was a statesman, scholar, and spiritual writer. Gregory's work was to bring both the secular and ecclesiastical orders into contact with spiritual inspiration — both a politician and a mystic. He did more than anyone else before Charlemagne to ensure that the Rule of St Benedict became the normal Roman monastic rule in use in the West. The life of St Benedict, the second of the *Dialogues*, is attributed to Gregory, although some scholars doubt the attribution. Nonetheless, the *Life* is full of detail that seems to suggest close knowledge of Benedict's life. Gregory's *Pastoral Care*, as we shall see later, still has much to say to leaders in Benedictine education. He also did much to nurture the culture of reading and, as Raymond Studzinski has pointed out, he stressed that learning is a communal activity: "He puts emphasis on the role of the community in coming to a fuller understanding of the meaning of the Scriptures, for he finds that preaching to the community is the occasion for his gaining insight. 'For I know that in the presence of my brothers and sisters I have very often understood many things in the sacred text that I could not understand alone.'"[32] Gregory also promoted the four senses, or levels of reading, in Scripture: literal, allegorical, moral (or tropological), and anagogical.

St Bede the Venerable (672/673–735)

The Venerable Bede, as he is also called, was an Anglo-Saxon monk of the twin monastery of Wearmouth-Jarrow, in the then-Saxon kingdom of Northumbria. He is often called the father of English history, on account of the impact of his most famous work, the *Historia ecclesiastica gentis Anglorum*, or *Ecclesiastical History of the English People* (731). He wrote over sixty books, on an immense range of topics, covering grammar, musical meter, biography, astronomy, architecture, and orthography; some of these were essentially textbooks for the classroom. He wrote in both Latin and Anglo-Saxon, and he was undoubtedly the most learned man of the Dark Ages between the fall of Rome and the rise of medieval Europe. David Knowles, one of the foremost modern Benedictine historians, goes so far as to say: "in his learning, in his candor, and in his art Bede is without rival in the Middle Ages. Among the world's great historians he has perhaps most kinship with the father of Greek history, Herodotus."[33]

We can see in Bede the emergence of a personality, both English and Benedictine, that was to make an indelible impression on what

---

32 Studzinski, 130.
33 Knowles, *Saints and Scholars*, 17.

in later times we come to see as the English character: resolutely empirical, restlessly curious, skillfully amateur, and with a solid sanity of outlook. As a historian, Bede seems always asking what actually happened and when, making history rather than myth: "There is no brilliance in Bede, but much steady clarity; no overtones and undertones, no subtle intuition, no twilight mystery, no lightning flash of genius. He lives and writes in the noonday sunshine."[34] The particular combination of the Germanic and the Roman, as distinct from the British and Celtic, is what we see emerging in Bede.

As a model for Benedictine educators, Bede reminds us that lucidity and clarity in the mind of the teacher can pass themselves on to the pupil; and if the teacher does not have lucidity and clarity, the pupil may not find them of his own accord. A pupil of Bede taught Alcuin, who was to serve Charlemagne's educational project, a fact that reminds us that as teachers we are links in a chain of influence. Abbot Cuthbert Butler reminds us of another feature of Bede that can be a model for teachers, quoting Bede, writing of himself, who, "amidst the observance of regular discipline and the daily care of singing in the church, always took delight in learning, teaching, and writing."[35] It is this delight that gives life to both teachers and pupils.

St Anselm of Canterbury (c. 1033–1109)

Anselm was born at Aosta, now in Italy, and became a monk at Bec in France. He became Archbishop of Canterbury in 1093, succeeding Lanfranc, and served under William (II) Rufus and Henry I, both of whom he opposed. His years as archbishop were very difficult, as Kings William and Henry pushed their claims of rights over the Church, including the right to appoint ("invest") bishops. Anselm was exiled twice, but he was ultimately quite successful in preserving and extending the authority of Canterbury within the English Church and against state interference.

---

34   Ibid.
35   Butler, 337.

Anselm was sixty years old when he became Archbishop of Canterbury. While at Bec, where he became abbot in 1079, Anselm wrote a number of highly significant philosophical and theological works, and Bec became the most important center of learning in Europe under his leadership and the power of his example. It is generally understood that Anselm's was the greatest intellect in all the years between St Augustine and St Thomas Aquinas. It was at Bec that he conceived his famous ontological argument for the existence of God, and wrote the famous phrases *fides quaerens intellectum* (faith seeking understanding) and *credo ut intelligam* (I believe in order to understand). Faith precedes understanding, not the other way around, says Anselm, following Augustine. It is a fascinating fact that in his explanation of the capacities and uses of human reason, Anselm, a Benedictine, is called "the father of scholasticism,"[36] the theology and philosophy that owed so much to the friars. Although his ontological argument has provoked much controversy and contradiction, it has continued to intrigue philosophers into modern times.

David Knowles has written that Anselm "is one of the two or three men in the course of fourteen centuries who have seemed to come nearest to the Benedictine ideal. The Venerable Bede is another, and a composite character-photograph of the two would make any description of the type unnecessary."[37] Anselm seems to have had a very attractive personality, and a gentle approach to discipline based on knowledge of the individual personalities of his monks: "Simplicity, humanity, gentleness allied to strength, a clear and sane mind, and a capacity to give and receive love, are all distinguishing traits of the abbot of Bec."[38] Such qualities, in addition to scholarship and continuing intellectual curiosity, make for an ideal Benedictine teacher.

---

36 Although we sometimes see scholasticism as a break with the wisdom tradition of antiquity, it is also interesting that the greatest of the scholastics or "schoolmen," Thomas Aquinas, received his early education at Monte Cassino.

37 Knowles, *Saints and Scholars*, 31.

38 Ibid., 31–2.

St Hildegard of Bingen (1098–1179)

Hildegard, a German abbess of aristocratic family, was known as the Sibyl of the Rhine. She was one of the most extraordinarily able persons of the High Middle Ages. She recorded, from her middle age, visions she had received since childhood, and wrote scientific and medical works, letters, poetry, drama, and music. A nun from the age of fourteen, she was elected prioress of the convent at Disibodenberg, eventually establishing an independent community of women at Rupertsberg. This was unusual, and opposed by authority at the time, as communities of women were normally under the ultimate control of an abbot. She was named a Doctor of the Church by Pope Benedict XVI in 2012, one of only four women among thirty-five people with that title. Hildegard also founded a second convent at Eibingen. She corresponded with popes, emperors, abbesses, and abbots, including Bernard of Clairvaux.

She wrote down her visions as visionary theology, full of symbolism of salvation, redemption, and the moral life. Her first work, *Scivias*, was approved by Eugenius III, the first Cistercian pope. In her last and longest visionary work, the *Liber Divinorum Operum*, she makes much use of the word *viriditas* (greenness), a word also found in Gregory's *Moralia in Job*, with which Hildegard would have been familiar. The idea of *viriditas* in Gregory is based on imagery of God's word bringing forth natural life amid drought, symbolizing how God brings about growth in the spiritual life of the Church. *Viriditas* is also a reflection of God's redemptive power. Hildegard uses the image of *viriditas* in her poetry and her music, and it connects with her great knowledge of herbs and natural history. *Viriditas* in Hildegard thus represents a holistic sense of the place of man with respect to God and creation, and the unity of all three.

Hildegard was a prolific polymath. Since she was a woman, it is unlikely that she would have been schooled in the liberal arts and it may be partly for that reason that her learning has the freedom of the autodidact, and the energy and creativity of the artist. The fact that she conducted four preaching tours, and denounced clerical corruption, is highly unusual for a woman of the time, since women were formally prohibited from public preaching. There seems to have been always something self-evidently valuable about Hildegard's work. She represents the ability of Benedictine life to accommodate new and authentic forms of human creativity, and the importance of the connectedness of all things, especially knowledge, wisdom, the spiritual life, and the natural world. As a teacher, she represents the integrated mind that teachers should model to pupils.

St Bernard of Clairvaux (1090–1153)

Bernard became a monk of Citeaux, near Dijon. The Cistercians, who came to be known as the white monks, were a reform of the Benedictines, or black monks. The founder of the Cistercians, Robert of Molesme, wanted to return to a more rigorous interpretation of the Rule of St Benedict than had become the norm. Bernard himself was to found the abbey of Clairvaux, and he became involved in controversy with the abbey of Cluny, which represented a very different version of monastic life, in contrast to the asceticism of Clairvaux. The Cistercians placed emphasis on work, particularly agriculture, as well as study, and their tendency to found offshoots of monasteries meant that the white monks would make a profound impact on the landscape of Europe in the centuries to come.

Bernard was born of a noble, military Burgundian family in a time when the Middle Ages were achieving a developed sense of the human individual and the value of human feelings. The theology of marriage and the literature of courtly love both reflected a sense of the importance of human experience. Bernard's spiritual writings similarly place an emphasis on the experience of the heart rather than the understanding of the intellect. He opposed the growing spirit of scholasticism, and successfully debated with Peter Abelard. In contrast to the *"credo ut intelligam"* of Anselm, Bernard preferred *"credo ut experiar"* — "I believe in order to experience." The difference is merely one of emphasis, however; in opposing the overstatement of the capacities of human reason,

Bernard was a highly capable reasoner himself. He also had an enormous capacity for action as well as for contemplation; his is a practical mysticism.

Bernard preached in favor of the First Crusade, but from the point of view of a chivalrous idealism. He saw his own monasteries as fortresses of peace, and his monks as an army of peace. His writings speak of the soul's relationship with God in the terms of human, even romantic love, most notably in his sermons on *The Song of Songs*, and it is in his showing how the self finds fulfillment only in the great depths of the love of God that he is a source of inspiration for teachers in a self-dominated age.

CHAPTER 3

Transformation

CONVERSATIO MORUM

The Benedictine religious makes vows of obedience, stability and *conversatio morum*, all three implying commitment to a particular community. For Thomas Merton, *conversatio morum* was the "most mysterious" of the vows. The term is usually left in Latin because it is so difficult to translate fully; it is variously rendered "conversion of morals," "conversion of manners," and "conversion to the monastic way of living." Later versions of the *Rule* used *"conversio"* rather than *"conversatio,"* but something is lost in the shorter form: "Whatever its exact meaning, *conversatio* implies process. The last four letters of the word (*-atio*) are a standard Latin suffix used to give it an ongoing and repetitive force: something that does not happen just once, but again and again."[1] The commitment to *conversatio* is then a commitment to living the religious life of Gospel values ever more fully and completely; a habituation to a way of living in a particular place and with a particular group of people; a homecoming in a house that leads to heaven, our true home. As a dynamic process in the *schola dominici servitii, conversatio* implies an education in a vocation of service, a remaking of the self that Terence Kardong says shows the influence of the Greek Church Fathers: "one of the major themes of Greek spirituality was the transformation of the individual into the image of God. They did not even hesitate to call it *theopoesis*, which means 'becoming godly.'"[2] The Benedictine genius, however, is to make the anticipation of heaven a very earthly process.

---

1 Terrence Kardong, *The Benedictines* (Dublin: Dominican Publications, 1988), 95.

2 Ibid., 96.

The Benedictine "school of the Lord's service" is a real project
in space and time. The transformative schooling of *conversatio*
makes real the life of the Gospel; it is not satisfied with abstract
theory, or mere intention. It is also a recognition of the reality of
human nature, within the terms of which we cannot avoid living — as Benedict's Rule, in so many places, explicitly recognizes.
At the same time as he actively pursues sanctity, the monk is
devoted to becoming as human as possible, fulfilling his God-given
humanity. An essential part of this humanity is living with others,
to be found in community but also in the radical solitude of the
hermit's life, if Thomas Merton's experience is any guide. Merton
entitled his last journal *Vow of Conversation*, in a play on another
sense of *conversatio*, which thus implies a dialogue, a speaking and
listening process. Conversation, then, is a recognition of the self
and its limits in a world of other selves, including that of God. This
recognition is the ground and nature of love, which can only exist
when the reality of other selves is felt and understood. Education
in *conversatio*, in the reality of community living, is thus a process
of dialogue with others, including those who speak to us through
texts both humane and divine — other people and God Himself.
In this way, as Merton shows us, even the eremitic reader and
writer can experience communion with God, and with others.

Formation, a word at the heart of Catholic education, takes
a number of prefixes, all of which are relevant to the process
that *conversatio* implies. *Formation* implies a kind of molding to
a preconceived image of the human person, but a problem with
this metaphor is that it encourages viewing of the person being
formed in the role of patient rather than actor: as though formation were something done to us in a way that takes no account of
our human freedom. Such a view is also present — even more so
perhaps — when *formation* is combined with *con-*: we are *conformed*
or we *conform* to the way of life given to us, as if the community
were an authoritarian state. Such a view would fit well with an
idea of education as *reformation*, with pupils seen as inherently
corrupt and fallen until remade under dogma and the threat of the
strap into half-decent human beings who bow to the authority of

the Church. But this is a parody of Christian living and Christian education, however much in the past the Church has descended into it. We may also understand "formation" as involving a receptivity to God acting in our lives, and of "conforming" as allowing God's acting through a community of others. Even the word *reformation* can encompass of the remaking of our selves when broken, a "making again" that says none of us is ever beyond repair. The word *transformation,* however, seems to come nearest to the depths (or heights) of what is implied in *conversatio*: the capacity for transcendence, for crossing over into new life, even if we spend this life on the crossing itself, the place of intersection.

We have called *conversatio* a process of homecoming, but it is so in the sense that Chesterton described it: a process of going around the whole world and returning to know the place for the first time. It is more an interior journey than an outward one, which is why it can happen in a monastic enclosure, for *conversatio* is a way of liberation and, as such, stands for a pedagogy of liberation. But where educationalists such as Freire[3] and Illich[4] have modeled their educational theories on ideologies of political and social freedom, Benedictine Catholic education takes as its inspiration the Gospel of spiritual freedom. As Thomas Merton puts it, "Life consists in learning to live on one's own, spontaneous, freewheeling: to do this one must recognize what is one's own — be familiar and at home with oneself."[5] The transformation of the Christian life may involve the dramatic, but it might also be (and this is the more likely in the reality of the monastic setting) a process of lifelong learning, a gradual homecoming of the self as it more perfectly realizes its human freedom: "Education in this sense means more than learning; and for such an education, one is awarded no degree. One graduates by rising from the dead."[6] Transformation is in the end resurrection, the new self in Christ,

3   Cf. Paulo Freire, *Pedagogy of the Oppressed* (1970).
4   Cf. Ivan Illich, *Deschooling Society* (1971).
5   Thomas Merton, "Learning to Live," in *Spiritual Master: The Essential Writings,* ed. Lawrence Cunningham (New York: Paulist Press, 1992), 358.
6   Ibid., 359.

transfigured and transcendent. Like the risen Jesus of the Gospels, it is both the same and utterly changed.

Another way of describing this kind of education is as an education of the heart. The origin of the Benedictine way in antiquity means that the ground of the essential human self is likely to be spoken of in terms of the heart rather than the mind (of modernity) or the brain (in postmodernity). The conversion of the heart is not only towards God but also towards a more complete humanity — more complete than a word like *mind* or *brain* would indicate. Conversion of life is growth in love, and so the process of learning, of education, is a relational one that arises from a community of persons. Paradoxically, says Maria Lichtmann, "transformation happens only when formation *breaks down*."[7] This implies a "change of heart," some kind of crisis, or *crux* — even an *agony*: "Deep learning is really about change of heart, what Jesus called *metanoia*. Often translated to mean 'repentance,' *metanoia* also means breaking open your heart or having it broken, transcending your ordinary view of reality. *Metanoia* is a way out of impasse. This kind of learning may happen only a few times in our lifetime, where we are utterly converted to a new way of seeing and of being."[8] As we have said, *metanoia* may be sudden and dramatic, but it can contain a lifetime; similarly, a lifetime may be a process of *metanoia*, the education of the human heart. It is in recognizing this perspective on education, a perspective *sub specie aeternitatis*, that the Benedictine teacher sees through the learning process in itself to what is beyond.

BENEDICTINE EDUCATIONAL VALUES

In recent years, Benedictine educational institutions have attempted to articulate the values at the heart of the Rule of St Benedict, which a Benedictine education seeks to pass on as valuable for Christian, human living. Characteristically, there is no

---

7   Maria Lichtmann, *The Teacher's Way: Teaching and the Contemplative Life* (New York: Paulist Press), 120.

8   Ibid., 88.

standard formulation of Benedictine values, although there is considerable overlap among various formulations. The effect of the emphasis on these values, which constitute the Benedictine *ethos*, is to stress the experiential nature of Benedictine education. Thus, Benedictine education relies very much on the local character of its living-out in a real place, in a real community, in real time. It is dependent on the *mores*, the way of doing things *here*. As such, it is reliant on particular customs and traditions which, without the concomitant emphasis on *conversatio* as the spirit of conversion, could become hidebound and formulaic, unable to respond to the spirit of the times. "Flexibility" is at the heart of the Rule, although this could not be called a "value"; it is not inherently valuable in itself. Many Benedictine institutions include the following among their core values, which are also hallmarks or characteristics: hospitality, stewardship, listening, and community. Prayer, or worship, and balance or moderation also are often mentioned; stability might appear, as does humility, and as do respect and integrity. "The Ten Hallmarks of a Benedictine Educational Institution" mentioned above, developed by the North American Association of Benedictine Colleges and Universities (ABCU), is notable for its clarity and completeness, and it is one of surprisingly few lists that include *conversatio morum*.

How does this transformative "way of doing things here," in a real place and in real time, work itself out in more detail? One way, developed in some depth by the Manquehue Apostolic Movement (MAM)[9] of Chile, is formed around a drawing-out of the significance of Benedict's phrase "a school of the Lord's service," the key words being *school, Lord*, and *service*.

1. Lord

The call of the Lord is the starting point for what we do. St Benedict asks us "to prefer nothing to Christ," and from this

---

9 Since its founding as a lay community in 1977, by Jose Manuel Eguiguren Guzman, MAM has grown to include 1,500 members, including a core group of 40 oblates, responsible for schools teaching some 4,000 pupils.

preferential option all other things flow. In the love of God begins our love for others, the motive of education for living. The call of the Lord puts prayer and worship at the heart of our education, since without this act of relationship to God the rest of what we do lacks meaning. The relationship with God that comes through prayer is the beginning of the way of humility, which we might see as the Lord's method of teaching us, as it is our method of teaching others. Whether communal acts of prayer, silence, worship, or reverence are made at the beginning of each lesson, once a day, or once a week, they will include all pupils and all teachers — and yet it is recognized that each individual will be in his own place in the spiritual life. This is a sensitivity to the times. Nowadays, not all teachers in Benedictine schools are monastics; not all are Catholics or Christians, or have any particular religious faith at all. But they must all be accepted as equals by virtue of their calling, and their humanity. Similarly, not all pupils in Benedictine schools will be Catholics or Christians of other denominations, but they are united and equal as children of God.

2. *School*

The love of God means for us the love of neighbor, and this is the origin of our conception of Christian community, the pattern for the Benedictine school. The school may be the first experience, for new pupils and new teachers, of a community that defines itself in love. School workplaces that define themselves by "success" (high exam results, entrance to top universities, lucrative career prospects) may or may not be founded in love, just as in fractured families the members may profess deep affection for each other while living atomized and self-centered lives: a Benedictine school may offer a new and challenging model of community. In a fast-moving and rapidly changing world, the characteristic of stability offers a model of commitment to others, and a recognition of the reality of human existence as one of interdependence and cooperation. The school itself will embody a commitment to its own traditions of value: learning, scholarship, a culture of reading, discourse, discussion, and debate, the interplay of word and Word in the contemplation of creation. In the spirit of hospitality, it will be an open community, welcoming to those who come to it for long or short periods of time, seeing Christ in the face of a stranger or the familiar person. The experience of community for both teacher and pupil is also the experience of the workings of balance and moderation, of the relative needs of "I" and "you," of learning that others are not simply objects in my existence, but subjects in their own.

3. Service

Benedictine education as an experience of God in Christ and others will awake in teacher and pupil a response, as to a call. "What, exactly, am I doing; what am I for?" asks the teacher. "What am I to do; who will I be when I grow up?" asks the pupil. Teachers model both service and vocation to pupils in a profession[10] that is a commitment to others, to learning and to a subject of inquiry. Vocation is defined by Frederick Buechner as "the place where your deep gladness and the world's deep hunger meet";[11] teachers frequently teach as a way of continuing their relationship with a subject they discovered as students, a subject that they enjoy and have come to love. They meet the hunger of pupils for both joy and meaning. This is common to all teachers, but Christian teachers have come to see through their subject a vision of God and of humanity, and this will be their motive for service, a sharing of gifts. Education is about meeting the needs of others; wise teachers will be aware of their own needs, their own shortcomings, and will be attentive to the wisdom of the young. Teaching and learning become a mutual exchange of gifts between persons. Pupils will have opportunities to serve each other, and others beyond the school, as a way of learning how to serve. Independently of the relative merits of various professions, careers, or forms of employment, the idea of vocation, coming

---

10   The word has monastic origins, later taken up by the universities, and is associated with professing vows, making a commitment.

11   Cf. Frederick Buechner, *Wishful Thinking: A Seeker's ABC* (1973).

from both God and others, should help pupils to inform the choices they make.

*   *   *

The Manquehue model sees six Benedictine values informing the character of the "school of the Lord's service" and the persons who make it what it is; they can be seen as characteristics of Benedictine teachers and pupils: listening, welcoming (*acogida* in Spanish), mission, order, stability, and the spirit of conversion. Manquehue has posed the question whether education is for *domestication* or *liberation*. Is it to form solid citizens, who behave well and cause no trouble to others, who work hard and contribute their fair share? Obviously, there is much to be said for this conception of a well-educated person. But the way of the Gospel also suggests that education should form people who are free to make a difference, to transform their own lives and the lives of those whom they touch. They can learn to adopt a critical awareness of their surroundings, a sensitivity to the plight of the poor; they become equipped to take prophetic actions. Wisdom teaches us that at the deepest level, oppositions disappear; *domestication* and *liberation* can be seen as two sides of the same coin. To be at home with oneself, and at home with one's place in the world, is also freedom if it is accepted in the spirit of the Lord's service. The spirit of *conversatio morum* is, after all, a dedication to a certain kind of enclosure, a way of life in a particular place and time. On the other hand, *conversatio* implies also an openness to constant renewal and acceptance of the call of the Lord's service, wherever it might lead.

THE PURSUIT OF WISDOM

How is it possible to offer to the modern world an education based on ancient wisdom? Such an approach seems not only counter-cultural but quixotic. Benedictine schools are mainly for fee-paying parents, most of whom would likely flee from the idea that their children should become monastics. They want them to be fitted for the world and able to find at least their fair share of success and happiness in worldly terms. It would be a brave headmaster who would quote this from Thomas Merton to an audience of prospective parents:

> A few years ago a man who was compiling a book entitled *Success* wrote and asked me to contribute a statement on how I got to be a success. I replied indignantly that I was not able to consider myself a success in any terms that had a meaning to me. I swore I had spent my life strenuously avoiding success. If it so happened that I had once written a best seller, this was a pure accident, due to inattention and naiveté and I would take very good care never to do the same again. If I had a message to my contemporaries, I said, it was surely this: Be anything you like, be madmen, drunks, and bastards of every shape and form, but at all costs avoid one thing: success. I heard no more from him and I am not aware that my reply was published with the other testimonials.[12]

What Merton is rejecting here, of course, is the calculation of success that is made in worldly terms, once looked down upon as "bourgeois." Success is defined in terms of income, status, competition and how we appear to our peers. Merton is aware of how dangerous such a calculus is to the health of the soul. It is the opposite of the realism that St Benedict offers in the path of humility. A realistic approach to human life will take account of the presence of failure in each human person, and the fact that anything of value that a person achieves is due to God working through our weakness. That the wisdom of God is foolishness to man is no new insight, and yet what parents do not wish their child happy?

"Where is the wisdom we have lost in knowledge? / Where is the knowledge we have lost in information?"[13] So T.S. Eliot

12   Merton, "Learning to Live," in *Spiritual Master*, 364–65.
13   T.S Eliot, "Choruses from 'The Rock,'" in *The Complete Poems and Plays of T. S. Eliot* (London: Faber and Faber, 1969), 147.

encapsulates the descent from the wisdom of the ancients, through the knowledge of the medievals, to the information age of modernity. Where once the highest reaches of education were to cultivate the things of the heart (to be Aristotelian) or the head (to be Platonic), in modernity, the age of consumption, the promise of education is largely to impart the means for the satisfaction of the will and appetite of *homo economicus*, to prepare for the illusory freedom of choice among distractions. It is not clear whether most parents really believe this, however keen they might be to give their children what their children want. In a culture where all things, including often people, are reduced to commodities, Benedictine education reveals the sacredness in all created things. Thomas Merton makes the point that both the monastery and university (in the earliest times inhabited by monks, as well as friars and clerks) teach "not so much by imparting information as by bringing the clerk (in the university) or the monk (in the monastery) to direct contact with 'the beginning,' the archetypical paradise world."[14] At their highest, both the scholastic pursuit of *scientia* (intellectual knowledge) and the monastic pursuit of *sapientia* (mystical contemplation) can lead to wisdom. A learning fired by faith can thus lead to a greater personal fulfillment, with the prospect of real happiness rather than the skills to manipulate information, or heartlessly negotiate the increasingly precarious world of employment: "If you are too intent on winning, you will never enjoy playing. If you are too obsessed with success, you will forget to live."[15] The transformation promised in an education based on wisdom is of an individual into a person, loved by God and capable of loving others.

"The only wisdom we can hope to acquire / Is the wisdom of humility: humility is endless,"[16] says Eliot, echoing what St Benedict tells us, that humility is a sure path into the infinite, which is love. And yet St Benedict's central virtue is much misunderstood

14   Merton, "Learning to Live," in *Spiritual Master*, 361.
15   Ibid., 365.
16   T. S. Eliot, "East Coker," in *Complete Poems and Plays*, 179.

in modernity as a denial of the self, of the good, a kind of life-hating pretense that we are smaller than we really are. Where is humility in our modern politics, commerce, and cult of celebrity? Actually, as we shall see later, it probably does exist there, but hidden beneath the false vision of success as based on *ego*, the conscious and constant projection of self-will. For St Benedict, by contrast, humility is the avoidance of all false and delusional conceptions of the self. As the etymology of the word suggests, it begins with the sense that we begin as earth (*humus*) and will return to the earth; we are only more than earth through the creative will beyond ourselves, which is God. This is the opposite of the claim that we are less than we are. As Bishop Fulton J. Sheen once put it, humility is not about pretending you are five feet tall when you are six feet; it is about seeing yourself as you really are. "Know thyself" is one of the most ancient philosophical insights, coming to us from ancient Egypt, via ancient Greece. St Benedict shows us that knowing ourselves as we really are is about recognizing and understanding our weakness. Only thus can we sympathize, and empathize, with the weakness of others. Only thus can we forgive and be forgiven, and form true relationships with God and other people. Paradoxically, humility is the way to real strength, a transformation in the power of God's love, enabling us to transcend what Christ meant by "the world."

Thus, humility — St Benedict's word for wisdom — makes all things possible. The way of descent, to the ground of our being, is also the way of ascent to God. The monastic life of *conversatio morum* is the way of humility, and St Benedict conceives of this way as a ladder with twelve steps, taking us ever higher towards heaven: "Our proud attempts at upward climbing will really bring us down, whereas to step downward in humility is the way to lift our spirit up towards God" (*RB* 7:7). In the Rule's chapter on humility, Benedict uses the word *cor* (heart) nine times; frequently, the word appears in a quotation from scripture. An education in humility is an education of the heart more than of the mind, and in this humility poses a distinct challenge to post-Cartesian modernity, where the head, the mind (or, perhaps, the brain of neuroscience) is the center of our being. The ways of the heart are more akin to intuitive living, the way of poetry, in the sense we have seen identified by Newman, whose motto as Cardinal was "*cor ad cor loquitur,*" sometimes rendered as "heart speaks to heart." Humility, like poetry, is a way of seeing life in the simplicity and power of its significant details: the flight of a bird, the movement of wind and trees, the taste of each bite of food, the smile of another person. It is an attentiveness to the reality of the world and the feeling self, and, through the extension made possible by love, to other feeling selves. It is the avoidance of all pretense, all artifice, all illusion and delusion, and to pursue the way of humility is to work to reduce the power of self-delusion, in a constant opening of ourselves to reality. Since God is ultimate reality, the most real thing, progress in humility enables us to be ever more receptive to him and what he seeks to do in our lives.

A problem with education for utility — schooling and degree-level education that seeks to impart skills so that the young can be useful in economic terms — is that what is useful is increasingly hard to discern in a fast-moving and shifting economy. Often, the skills and knowledge of school are of little use in the real world, and the argument made in response by educationalists and those in the world of commerce and industry is that education should be more relevant, and adjust to the demands of economic necessity. In fact the answer seems rather to be to avoid further engagement with ephemeral "skills" and focus on character and the development of the young as persons. The deep learning of Benedictine education, in addressing the formation of the heart in what can satisfy human beings' deepest desires, will make for happier individuals and a happier society. In what are human beings most likely to find meaning, purpose, and joy? It won't be in the sugar-coated, brightly colored, and noisy ephemera of a diabetic culture hooked on commodities. It will be in enduring relationships, a creativity of mind and heart, a grounding in the natural world, and a sense of value in being of service to others: all these are contingent upon some kind of relationship with the divine. The pursuit of wisdom, the path of humility, forms persons capable of true happiness, which is what most parents (when put to it) most desire for their children. In placing humility at the center of Benedictine education, as it is for Benedictine values for living, we make possible the transformation of all human desire into (to borrow Leclercq's phrase) the love of learning and the desire for God.[17]

TRANSFORMING SCHOOLS

If Benedictine schools transform the lives of those who study and teach in them, they are also influenced, to some extent, by the world in which they exist: this is true even as, over time, they have some permanent effect on that world. Transformation, understood in *conversatio*, a dialogue of conversation, is an exchange of gifts, a spiritual and material commerce between the community of prayer and the world close to but beyond the cloister. Benedictine schools are affected inevitably by local norms, just as they serve local needs: this is entirely to be expected in a spiritual tradition that is rooted in place and time. In England, for example, the Benedictine schools readily absorbed the public school tradition, especially as it was reformed and expanded in the nineteenth century, when English Catholics were becoming increasingly free of the legal handicaps imposed on them after the Protestant Reformation. Perhaps this transformation happened partly because, as we have said above, many of the (now-Anglican) original public schools, having their origins in the Catholic Middle Ages, retained a certain monastic character, but no doubt another factor, characteristic of Benedictine foundations, was a symbiosis with the environment. A consequence of the traditional self-contained independence of Benedictine houses is that their schools (as "works" of the monasteries) provide an income from privately paid fees, rather than in grants from the local or national state. This financial need in turn

17 This focus on humility as a motive for a transformative engagement with the world corresponds to building what Gerald Grace has called "Spiritual Capital" in schools. See chapters 1 to 3 in Grace, *Faith, Mission and Challenge in Catholic Schools* (Abingdon, Oxon: Routledge, 2016).

provides a number of challenges for Benedictine schools operating within the economic and educational norms of the twenty-first century, and to these challenges we shall return.

For many Benedictine schools today, there is an ongoing transformation from being schools with Benedictines to being Benedictine schools. Partly, this is due to the decline in monastic vocations leading to the widening of lay involvement in the leadership of Benedictine schools, and to a more conscious and deliberate development of a Benedictine approach to learning. However, nowhere has this conscious development been carried out more thoroughly and systematically than in the educational and curricular projects of the Manquehue Apostolic Movement (MAM), itself conceived from the first as a lay Benedictine movement, in Chile. First, the MAM educational vision includes a specific view of Man, a Christian anthropology, that sees the human as "created, fallen, redeemed," so requiring of pupils and teachers a disposition to listen and attend to God, especially in the experience of Scripture (through *lectio divina*). The second aspect of the MAM educational vision is that the path to God, which for each person is a unique vocation, can only be worked out in community. Third, the teaching and learning ethos, which emerges from a Christian anthropology and a community-based sense of individual vocation, is embodied in the concept of *tutoría*; this is a particular kind of master-disciple relationship, infused with spiritual friendship, as the basis for mission and service.[18] The whole of this three-part educational vision (corresponding as it does to the three points of LORD, SCHOOL, and SERVICE, discussed above) is combined in the central Benedictine virtue of *humility*, and involves a constant process of *conversion*.

The Manquehue schools, three day schools within the large modern city of Santiago, Chile, seek to have an impact in serving the larger city-community in which they exist. So also does another South American Benedictine school, São Bento in Rio de

18 MAM is indebted for this idea, in particular, to St Aelred of Rievaulx (1110–1167), as it is to the English Benedictine tradition in general.

Janeiro, Brazil, founded in 1854, attached to a monastery founded in 1598. Service in the community is a part of every pupil's education. For example, *lectio* is linked to action on the streets of Rio. The pupils of the school tend to live in apartments, so contact with the earth, such as in planting trees, is promoted. In a home for the elderly, the young meet the old, and the elders give dancing lessons to the young, in an exchange of gifts. The pupils look after younger children in a day nursery. The commitment to transformation in these Benedictine schools is not simply carried out within the walls of the immediate school community, but manifests itself in, and is sustained by, the wider local community with which it lives. Benedictine transformation involves a receptivity, a welcoming hospitality, to the needs of the other, who comes as Christ in his need, to awaken the human heart to the new life of grace. The needs of others are themselves a gift to us.

A further powerful example of the way in which a Benedictine school devotes itself to the needs of the modern city is in St Benedict's Prep, a boys' day school, in Newark, New Jersey. The remarkable story of this school, and its readjustment in the face of a felt urban need emerging from the inner-city riots of 1967, is told in the film *The Rule* (2014), by filmmakers Marylou and Jerome Bonjiorno. The film reflects the drama of tension between the city of Man and the city of God, between the modern, temporal city and the eternal city of the Kingdom. As Fr Albert says in the film, "Any monastery is in dialogue with its locale," and the same may be said of the monastic school, as of the monastery. Newark Abbey and St Benedict's Prep took "a prophetic stance" in response to the inner city riots of 1967, and confronted the underlying local racism, even though tensions within the city were also played out in the monastery itself, some of the monks deciding to leave and find a new home elsewhere. In the context of continuing civil and familial breakdown, the school works to build "connectedness" among students, faculty, and monks, replacing the broken trust experienced by the students in their homes and families with a sense of human care and reliance on others. Often, before the students come to the school their emotional needs have not been met, and these needs are addressed as a necessary precursor to academic focus, in which the school is highly successful, as it is also in sport.

The story of St Benedict's Prep is a reminder that the life of St Benedict himself is a story of response to urban breakdown, and receptive engagement with the barbarians who both caused and were subject to the decay of Roman civility. The story also shows how the transformative effects of Benedictine educational engagement go both ways: the broken lives of the poor can be redemptive of the lives of the wealthy, including those who have spiritual wealth. The running of the school demands material and personal resources, but the spiritual life of the monastery is also partly sustained by the students in the school. St Benedict's Prep, like the monastery, is a sign of contradiction in the educational world of modern Western society, in showing that a Benedictine Catholic education is not something that can be easily measured as "effective and efficient" by criteria used in the secular world, even as it achieves a high degree of success in terms of college entrance and completion rates and national success on the sports field. Its real achievements lie, as the film suggests, in helping the young to find the spiritual resources to be faithful to others in their future adult lives.

Benedictine schools face contemporary challenges that provide an impetus to transformation. As we have noted, it is the nature of Benedictine life, including in its educational activity, to be diverse, organic, and inclined to take different forms depending on the particular territory a school or monastery inhabits. The Benedictine "Order" has no centralized structure dependent on a provincial hierarchy, as in Orders of modern foundation. The autonomy of individual monastic houses even within national and international groups (known as "congregations") means that the process of transformation is experienced very much at the local level, according to local needs and capabilities. Some Benedictine schools, especially in Europe, will find themselves in more remote places, and dependent on the custom of boarding schooling; but the escalating costs of such a schooling threaten to distance these places further from their localities or nationalities, and encourage a reliance on fee-paying parents from farther abroad. On the other hand, such schools can be places of stability in a rapidly changing and globalized world. City-based Benedictine schools might find more Catholic parents in the locality, sometimes in increasing numbers due to current migration patterns, but some Catholic parents might prefer non-Catholic fee-paying schools that appear to offer higher academic standards — which in turn encourages Benedictine schools to drive up their academic standards, perhaps at the expense of their pastoral value. Benedictine schools that are entirely or heavily reliant on fee income (as opposed to endowments or state funding) may become overly reliant on a non-Catholic or non-Christian school population, so that their Catholicity becomes a matter of concern to their leaders. On the other hand, Benedictine schools in some parts of the world have always been used to providing a Catholic education to a non-Christian, perhaps Muslim, population; these will face their own challenges, however. But whatever the particular, potentially transformative factors that operate on the school from external sources, it is the call to evangelization (including the New Evangelization of the once- or post-Christian) coming from the very heart of the Church in the modern world that Benedictine schools must now heed.

CHAPTER 4
Leadership

BENEDICT'S ABBOT

Any consideration of what St Benedict has to say about leadership will inevitably focus on what the Rule says about the abbot of the monastic community, although the chapters that relate to other leaders in the monastery, such as the Prior, the Cellarer, and the Deans, are also relevant in revealing the spirit of Benedictine leadership. We have mentioned that, before the pervasive influence in Western monasticism of the Rule of St Benedict, *regulae* for monastics usually proceeded from the abbot and carried his personal stamp. With the spread of the Rule of St Benedict, we see the development of a kind of constitutionalism, such that the document of the Rule binds both monk and abbot, and directs both. (A study of the influence of the Benedictine Rule in relation to Western political constitutionalism would be interesting, if outside the scope of the present study.) The characteristics of Christian leadership, in both Church and state as they developed through early and later medieval Europe, suggest the influence of Benedict's Rule, and that of other models rooted in the monastic tradition such as Gregory the Great's *Pastoral Rule*.

The abbot's authority, however, is something straight out of the ancient world, and particularly ancient Rome. The abbot is a *paterfamilias* who is entitled to expect, as a bottom line, the unquestioning obedience of his monks, a principle enshrined in one of the vows the monk makes as part of his full reception into monastic life.[1] In this respect, the Rule presents the abbot's authority in a way which is very unfamiliar, and uncongenial,

---

1 An engaging fictional representation of the challenges of obedience in a monastic community is given in Brian Moore's short novel *Catholics* (1972).

to us in modernity, where vows of obedience (such as of wives to husbands) seem of their nature to be wrong according to the canons of political correctness. The idea of unquestioning obedience to a superior has been in disrepute since the end of the Second World War, where the consequences of blindly following orders — albeit immoral ones — are all too evident. But the genius of St Benedict's approach seems to be in extending this commitment to obedience from, and to, particular persons, to a design for living in community — a design that is both the Rule itself and the spirit of mutual obedience (*RB* 71). This extension allows Benedict to conceive obedience as something more dynamic and creative than merely the effects of the exercise of authority.

The first part of the Rule to focus on the abbot is Chapter 2, on the gifts and abilities an abbot should possess. These might be summarized as follows:

- To represent Christ, and mold his own teaching to Christ's
- To be responsible for the souls of those he cares for
- To remain steadfast in Christ's teaching, even when it is unpopular
- To be a good example
- To speak so as to benefit others
- To avoid favoritism, and to love all
- To keep everything in order
- To use discretion and judgment, sometimes severe, sometimes gentle
- To avoid tolerating wrongdoing, but to nip things in the bud
- To be mindful that of those to whom much has been given much is expected
- To adapt to human nature and to the nature of individuals
- To avoid making excuses about lack of resources
- To be ready to give an account of himself

Benedict's thinking here emphasizes carrying out the duties of a position. The abbot exercises and embodies the *lordship* of Christ, even using as a title, *abba*, the intimate word which is used by

Christ of his Father. The abbot is certainly a governor and ruler. There is a double note of judgment; he is reminded that he is a judge and will himself be judged. He exercises discipline and might need to be severe in order to keep good order. This kind of abbot is in charge, makes the decisions, and must be decisive and capable of making clear and firm judgments. He is in control of himself and his own feelings. However, he must be skillful in the way he manages others, and we also see in this chapter the characteristic Benedictine note of humanity and love.

There is an interesting symbiosis here between authority and freedom. To start with, the abbot must have a sense of his own freedom so that he can use his discretion and come to conclusions, even when these come after freely given counsel from the community, as outlined in Chapter 3 of the Rule, an important counterpoint to Chapter 2. Benedict here makes clear to the abbot that he must *take responsibility*. As former Abbot Primate Notker Wolf has put it, "Leadership is about taking responsibility for people because of your position, a responsibility that cannot be ignored except at the expense of those you lead."[2] There is an ineradicable and non-delegable authority in the office the abbot holds: "However restrained and willing to co-operate a leader is, it must be clear who is in charge and bears the responsibility. It would be a capital error to bashfully deny one's authority or perhaps hide in the group and plead the collective vote, according to the motto 'That's what they wanted. I was not in favor, but I was powerless in the matter.'"[3]

More important, however, than the office the abbot holds is his need for an inner confidence and calm, which Notker Wolf calls "sovereignty," for Wolf the central leadership quality, which we might also call the self-possession that enables the loss of self: "I would define sovereignty as greatness manifested as modesty, as strength expressed as empathy and understanding, and as the inner freedom to defer one's own concerns and be of service.

2 Notker Wolf and Enrica Rosanna, *The Art of Leadership* (Collegeville, MN: Liturgical Press, 2013), 38.
3 Ibid., 43.

Sovereignty is, strictly speaking, the central concept of this book and basically also the main idea behind any form of leadership not founded on power."[4] Benedict's emphasis on authority, and its place in the lordship of Christ, might be seen as a counter to the *timocratic leadership* — rule by the rich and therefore powerful — very visible in Benedict's own time and culture. In contrast, Benedict's central injunction, "to prefer nothing to Christ," operates as much in his vision of leadership as in everything else.

The other part where Benedict discusses the abbot directly is Chapter 64. Some readers[5] have seen in this chapter a more mature voice speaking, less dependent on the Rule of the Master (on which Chapter 2 is heavily reliant) and evoking more the leader as *shepherd* rather than lord. (The distinction being made here between Chapters 2 and 64 is merely one of emphasis, however; the image of the shepherd is already present in Chapter 2, and Benedict returns to certain Chapter 2 themes, for example discretion, in Chapter 64.) Chapter 64 focuses more on the person than the place of the abbot, and looks at moral, human qualities that make for effective leadership. In electing an abbot, the community is enjoined to choose someone who will be

- dedicated to religious living
- a wise teacher
- a steward of souls
- helpful to others rather than a wielder of power over them
- chaste, sober, compassionate, and merciful
- a hater of vice and a lover of persons
- careful not to demand more than someone is capable of giving
- loved more than feared
- well-balanced and moderate
- able to exercise discretion in judgment
- inspiring for both the strong and the weak.

4   Ibid., 58.
5   Cf. Terrence Kardong, *Benedict Backwards: Reading the Rule in the 21st Century* (Collegeville, MN: Liturgical Press, 2017).

Here, Benedict speaks in a more humane register, and the chapter seems to show the fruits of personal experience. The cardinal virtues of temperance, fortitude, prudence, and justice are very present here, and the whole chapter suggests a concern less for community order than for human growth, with less of a need for a ruler than for a pastor. The realism in the images such as the rusty vessel and the bruised reed is striking and memorable, as is the adjuration to seek to be more loved than feared. This last imperative might be surprising if we think that Benedict is encouraging the abbot to indulge in *charismatic leadership* and create a cult of personality. But what Benedict seems to mean rather is that the abbot must enter into a relationship with the individual persons in his care, and to do this he must drive out fear, rather than use it as a management tool.

So, again, we might say in summary, we come to this theme in the Rule of humanity, in all the implications of the word. The Rule itself is a serious and sympathetic, orderly and flexible attempt to engage practically with the demands of human living in community, and the abbot himself, more than any others, must engage with this aspect of the spirit of the Rule. Notker Wolf has pointed to the importance of a "knowledge of human nature" in the abbot: "As a leader you have to respond to non-verbal signals; you must be able to see, for example, that this person is a troublemaker, that one will down sails at the first sign of headwind, and this other one has his eye on the top position — and to do so you need the kind of intuition that develops with experience."[6] Benedict is not starry-eyed about human nature, nor does he see it as inherently extremely limited; it is corrupt from Adam, but with a huge potential for good in Christ. For this reason, "people need freedom," says Notker Wolf, "especially when they are supposed to be producing good work." A leader needs then to "create an anxiety-free space" around people, and "[he] must discipline [himself] daily, hourly, to see them properly."[7] Shaping, moderating, and modifying human nature is part of the role of the leader:

6   Wolf and Rosanna, *The Art of Leadership*, 42.
7   Ibid., 18–19.

Finding the right note for criticism, however, requires immense sensitivity and great self-control, because criticism is always voiced in an already tense atmosphere and for the criticized person much more is at stake than just her professional competence with respect to the matter in hand. In his Rule, Benedict goes into more detail about correction than almost anything else, and what he says proves again and again to me that knowledge of human nature is not something that we have only acquired recently in our modern, psychologically enlightened era.[8]

HALLMARKS OF BENEDICTINE LEADERSHIP

Let us remind ourselves of the North American Association of Benedictine Colleges and Universities' Ten Core Values of a Benedictine Community:

1. Love
2. Prayer
3. Stability
4. *Conversatio morum*
5. Obedience
6. Discipline
7. Humility
8. Stewardship
9. Hospitality
10. Community

It is an interesting exercise to consider how these values might be applied to particular aspects of a Benedictine educational community, as to that community in general. What follows is an attempt to consider how these values are manifested in a Benedictine approach to leadership, as principally outlined in the office and qualities of the abbot. Relevant chapters from the Rule are indicated.

8 Ibid., 67.

1. LOVE *leads to a desire to promote the good of the other person. (RB 2, 27, 31, 44, 64)*

The abbot is seen as a father, teacher, and shepherd, and his love is both ordering and nurturing. The role of the Benedictine leader is like that of a parent, and his actions are like those of a loving one. He should seek more to be loved than feared (*RB* 64:15), and he adapts himself in a humane way to the natures of his charges (*RB* 2:23 ff.). He sees people as persons, not as a collective mass. As St Gregory first put it, he is *servus servorum Dei*, the servant of the servants of God, so he practices *servant leadership*. As shepherd, like St Peter, he is asked to feed the Lord's lambs and sheep, so he asks of each one, "What do you need?" He is sensitive to the way in which his own words and actions will be received. He avoids anger, since as St Paul tells us, love is not angry. He embodies benevolence, and he seeks virtues as well as skills. He is outward-focused and more interested in others than in himself, more aware of their dignity than his own. He respects the freedom of others, and he corrects out of love.

2. PRAYER *leads to a desire for good communication. (RB 2, 5, 6, 19, 20)*

The Benedictine leader is conceived of in the Rule as *a teacher with disciples*; the abbot is the chief teacher of the monastery. He teaches both adults and children. He teaches by word and example. "A person who wants to lead others has to master the art of conversation," says Notker Wolf.[9] The words with which he teaches find their character in the words of prayer, the words of the *opus Dei* and of *lectio divina*. His words give heart, they encourage, and they are spoken with courage. He speaks when it is necessary to do so, not when it is convenient; he is ready to speak of faults as well as of successes. His teaching edifies, builds up the community, exhorting, admonishing, asking, praising, and thanking. He guards the communal language, his own and that of others, in a speech which is plain and can be easily understood. He guards against negative speech or murmuring, and he ensures that the public

9   Ibid., 66.

language of the community is in harmony with its character. He creates with words lucidity and clarity, so as to reveal purposes and objectives. Like Christ, he speaks with authority, and he articulates the vision to which the community tends.

3. STABILITY *leads to the nurturing of a commitment to leading others.* *(RB 64, 66)*

A Benedictine leader, whether he leads the monastery itself or has a leadership role in the monastery, in its school, or in any other works of the monastery, will share in the commitment to the *stabilitas loci* of the monk, so that his life and work is bound up with the community, to the place and the people that constitute it. A Benedictine community requires much commitment, but it should be an enriching commitment, not a "burdensome" one. In avoiding placing excessive burdens on others, the leader should not overburden himself so that he experiences "burnout," since his commitment should last a significant time, which might even be lifelong. He is not a "workaholic"; he must not give the example that his work is everything, to the exclusion of life itself: work is a way to life, not a substitute for it. His commitment will entail his presence rather than his absence, and his presence should be evident in visibility, approachability, and generosity with time for anyone who seeks him. (He is cenobitic rather than vagrant.) He is committed to making the place the best it can be for those many who depend upon it, and he recognizes that the human gifts of all those within it take time to cultivate. He is committed to those he leads, especially when they fail.

4. CONVERSATIO MORUM *leads to a focus on constant improvement.* *(RB 2, 3, 7, 73)*

The Rule of St Benedict enjoins *leadership by example* (RB 2:12), and the example of how he lives his life is an important part of the teaching role of the Benedictine leader. He is open to development; he recognizes that he has never arrived as a leader, that he still has much to learn. He acts upon the need to learn and seeks to educate himself, partly by taking counsel of his colleagues. He is sympathetic to ideas of *transformational leadership*, and he can strike a good balance between permanence and change, recognizing that a living community cannot stand still. His leadership should be something that aids in forming his soul and the souls of others.

5. OBEDIENCE, *or listening, enables discretion. (RB 61, 64, 71)*

The Benedictine leader listens to develop good judgment (see Wolf and Rosanna, Chapter 11). He seeks to develop discretion in others. He expects cooperation from others and so does not have to ask for it. He practices mutual obedience and is responsive to the needs of others, but as a *sovereign leader* he is at no one's command. He is free to act on his conscience, and not inclined to give people what they want for an easy peace. He recognizes that in order to lead he must be able to follow, and that both *followership* and leadership require detachment from ego. He recognizes that leadership must be exercised *collectively*, and must be *distributed*. If a dean or a prior, he understands the need to obey. He has the discretion to see the limits of his own powers and abilities.

6. DISCIPLINE *leads to the maintenance and encouragement of high standards. (RB 22–30)*

The Benedictine leader maintains standards among those he leads. He is attentive to the norms and boundaries, and corrects those who stray from them. He does not avoid the difficult conversations but faces them with courage and calm, seeing that correction must build up the follower, not reduce him. He has self-discipline, so that he sees others as Christ sees them; he guards against negative motivations in himself. He is especially vigilant and active against murmuring, arrogance, and pride. He is ready to reprove where necessary. He nurtures an anxiety-free space in which people are ready to admit their mistakes. He has a sense of proportion. He will protect the community when necessary by "excommunicating" those who will not amend themselves, and he will remove from office those who cannot carry out their duties properly.

7. HUMILITY *leads to the exercise of the principle of subsidiarity.*
(RB 7)

He recognizes that he cannot do everything and must give
freedom of action with appropriate remits to those under him,
some of whom may also have a leadership role. He has a sense of
the appropriate levels at which certain decisions must be made.
Leadership is distributed through the community; the Rule speaks
of the abbot, and also of priors, deans, and cellarers (who have the
care of the goods of the monastery), all having leadership roles.
He can give and take responsibility. He admits his own faults and
errors. He avoids *charismatic leadership,* since this can lead to pride,
and he exemplifies Jim Collins's "Level 5 leadership."[10] He has the
inner calm of the sovereign leader, and he consults confidently,
seeking the advice of free-minded people.

8. STEWARDSHIP *leads to the building of trust. (RB 31, 32)*

As leader, he is aware that he will have to give an account of
what he has done, and of those in his care. He is aware of his lack
of possession, that what he has been given is held in trust. He
looks to trust those whom he leads, and they trust him to do
well by them, even when they do not particularly like what he
asks of them: they trust to his authority and experience, and his
motives. He has respect for the work of others, and he cultivates
their freedom. He takes note of the parables of the wicked tenants
and the unjust steward: he is aware of the temptation to theft, in
taking away what is not his; he is generous so that he will receive
generosity in turn; he makes things grow so that he may give
a good account of what has been entrusted to him. He avoids
over-burdening people, but cultivates their talents for their good
and the good of others. He recognizes that the work of others is
essential to their humanity and their self-actualization.

---

10   Jim Collins, "Level 5 Leadership: The Triumph of Humility and Fierce
Resolve," in *On Leadership* (Boston, MA: Harvard Business Review Press, 2011),
115–36.

9. HOSPITALITY *leads to a culture of receptivity. (RB 53, 61)*
He is open to others and avoids defensiveness. Like Love in
George Herbert's poem "Love III," he counters the feelings of unworthiness in others and puts them at their ease, as their servant. He
is aware of how the feeling of unworthiness can manifest itself in
stubbornness, defensiveness, and bitterness in those who are led.
The spirit of hospitality makes the leader receptive to ideas and perspectives from outside the Benedictine tradition, remembering from
the Rule (61:4) that those from outside may have a special mission
from Providence to bring a critical perspective on the monastery.

10. COMMUNITY *leads to an atmosphere of moderation. (RB 64)*
He is moderate in all things and a moderator within the community. He re-balances himself and others. He sees the community
as an organism rather than a mechanism. He is the *leader as wheel-
wright,*[11] adjusting spokes and spaces to make the team he leads most
effective. He is sensitive to the need for balance in people's lives:
between work and leisure, between the workplace and the home.
He knows that leadership in the community needs a community
culture supportive of the ideals of leadership. The leader must keep
all things within a sense of proportion; as Notker Wolf puts it: "People in leadership positions do indeed constantly need to maintain a
sense of proportion, to know whether a dispute is about something
substantial or there has been a totally unnecessary counterattack.
The former abbot general of the Trappists, the Argentinian Bernardo
Olivera, summed it up best with the ironic formula 'Blessed is he
who can distinguish one grain of sand from a mountain.'"[12]

LEADERSHIP HUMILITY

It is counter-cultural in an age in which it is typical for leaders to
make grandiose claims for themselves, but another way to look at

---

11 Cf. Keith Grint, *Leadership: A Very Short Introduction* (Oxford: Oxford
University Press, 2010), 104.
12 Wolf and Rosanna, 69–70.

Benedictine leadership is through the lens of the central Benedictine virtue of humility, as it is expressed in Chapter 7 of the Rule. If the abbot in the community does not possess humility then he is not setting the right example in the most important virtue. In Chapter 7, St Benedict speaks of humility as a ladder of ascent to God. What follows includes a very brief summary of what Benedict says about each step, and how it relates to leadership.

STEP 1: *Fear the Lord*

The first step of humility is to nurture an outward focus on others, starting with God. The leader needs to remind himself that he is not the center, and certainly is not God — rather, Christ is both: the leader keeps his gaze on him. The Gospel reminds us that the unjust judge fears neither God nor man; conversely, the just judge fears the Lord and respects man. In losing himself, the leader finds himself. St Gregory the Great's highly influential *Pastoral Rule* begins by talking about all the challenges that leadership poses for the soul for the leader. The careerist seeks leadership positions for himself rather than for the good he might do others; people will be reluctant to follow such a leader.

STEP 2: *Do not seek your own way*

Again, St Benedict reminds us that leadership is not about the leader, but about those whom he leads. It is natural that the leader seek his own way, but his decisions (decisions he should stick to once made) must be made on the basis of what is true and right, not what is convenient to the leader; thus his leadership is a loss of self. What the leader desires in his heart (in Latin *cor*, a word Benedict uses frequently: 37 times, or 57 if one includes derivative words such as *concordia, misericordia, discordia, corpus*, and *corporalis*) should be the common good. This will be determined on the basis of consultation and listening, but it will not necessarily be just what the majority want.

STEP 3: *Submit to superiors*

Egotistical leadership shows itself in an inability to follow another's leadership. St Benedict asks the abbot to follow, in humility, the lead of wisdom, even when it comes from the youngest members of the community. Conversely, leaders need the support of those who are led, for the good of the whole. Leadership never exists solely in one person in any real human community; the lead will come from various sources, and discernment will find out where the voice of leadership originates. Up to a point, we who are led should forgive the weaknesses of leaders, just as we who lead should forgive the weaknesses of those we lead. Leadership is a means to an end, which is the health of the group.

STEP 4: *Be patient*

For someone to be very long in a leadership position requires the development of resilience to inevitable adversity. Leaders can never please everyone all the time, nor should they attempt to please all. As part of his "Level 5 Leadership," Jim Collins encourages leaders to keep their focus, quietly and without ostentation, on the intended outcomes. The exercise of leadership — especially in the modern world — can easily succumb to the temptation of quick fixes and superficial, measurable results; in this way the dedicated careerist enables his rapid ascent up the greasy pole — which is very different from the ladder of humility. To use a metaphor from the old agricultural world, the straight furrow is ploughed by keeping one's eyes on the distant marker, at the end of the field; it takes a while to get there. Our brave new world thinks of machine-metaphors, with their implicit perfectibility, but humility and humanity teach us that this is an illusion. Leadership is more like cultivating a garden than fixing the car, and the leader should be steadfast in avoiding convenient illusions.

STEP 5: *Confess your faults*

Some leaders can start to believe their own propaganda. Humility teaches us not to inhabit a world of illusion, rather to keep our feet on the ground of reality. If we believe in our own perfection, or even perfectibility by our own efforts, we are unable to be truthful to others. If we admit our failings to others, we can build an "anxiety-free space" in which all can admit their weaknesses and seek the help of others in addressing them. This is Benedict's spirit of "fraternal correction." Leadership can bring intolerable stresses if we are unable to share our burdens and ask advice, and high-level leaders should always have mentors, friends to phone — human support outside the structures of management and accountability. Leaders should speak truth to their own power, not in order to ham-string themselves, but to keep developing.

STEP 6: *Accept hardships*

You really *shouldn't* want this job, says St Gregory in his *Pastoral Rule*, in so many words. Leadership will not be easy all the time, and at times it will bring difficult challenges to the spirit. The task of drawing out people's abilities, talents, creativity is beset with human frailty, failure, and all the admixture of human nature. Resilience is not so much the ability to stand up against what comes your way, but the ability to pick yourself up when you've been knocked down, to recover from failure. It is a paradox of failure that it can create opportunities for new growth.

STEP 7: *Recognize that others are better*

Good leadership shows itself in how well those around the leader are doing their jobs. To take two examples from ancient China: The Emperor Liu Bang, when asked why he was emperor (since he was not actually a noble by birth), asked in return, "What determines the strength of the wheel?"[13] It is not just the spokes, the collective resources of the group; it is also the spaces between

13   Grint, 104.

the spokes, the freedom for people to act for themselves. Lao Tzu speaks of the almost-invisible leader:

> The best rulers are those whom the people hardly know
>   exist.
> Next come rulers whom the people love and praise.
> After that come rulers whom the people fear.
> And the worst rulers are those whom the people despise.
> The ruler who does not trust the people will not be
>   trusted by the people.
> The best ruler stays in the background, and his voice is
>   rarely heard.
> When he accomplishes his task, and things go well,
> The people declare: it was we who did it by ourselves.[14]

Humility enables us to rely on others, and to avoid action or speech unless there is a good reason for it. Leadership can be about letting go, seeing when others are capable of their own freedom; when they are not thus capable, it should be about supporting them until they are.

STEP 8: *Keep to the rules of the place*

The leader might respond, "But I make the rules!" Perhaps. Once the rules are made, however, the leader must abide by them, if he expects others to do so. Nothing brings leadership into disrepute more quickly than the sense that there's one rule for them and another for us. Part of the constitutionalism of Benedict's Rule is the sense that the Rule is over the abbot, rather in the spirit of the medieval constitutionalism of Henry de Bracton, writing in the thirteenth century on English law: "The king is not above the law, but the law makes the king."[15] Ultimately, that which is above us is God. A salutary thought for a leader is that if he were

---

14   Wolf and Rosanna, 26.
15   Cf. Henry de Bracton (c. 1210–c. 1268), *De Legibus et Consuetudinibus Angliae* ("On the Laws and Customs of England").

to disappear tomorrow, many things would carry on just as well without him, even if not forever; the loss of a good leader will be felt at some point, but as a monk once remarked, "The monastery graveyard is full of indispensable monks..."

STEP 9: *Be careful of speech*

There is a school of thought holding that leaders are great talkers, naturally dominating the conversation or the room in which they find themselves. St Benedict seems to suggest something different. He is very much aware of the power of words to build up or to break down. Words can be misunderstood and misinterpreted. Language should be used with care, with an inclination to sparing use of words, aiming for clarity and a lack of ambiguity. Benedictine leaders need, perhaps, to listen more than speak, and like the best teachers they must have the highest regard for truth.

STEP 10: *Avoid easy laughter*

Some leaders maintain their position by pointing out, partly with mocking laughter, that no one else around is up to the job. Benedict's leader is no stage comedian, and the Roman respect for *gravitas* is very much felt. Alongside *gravitas* is the respect for *taciturnitas*; Chapter 6 of the Rule is subtitled "*De Taciturnitate*" — of silence. Leaders should appear serious-minded. Laughter in a community is often at someone's expense, but smiles and moderate laughter can communicate the joy of life (and the joy of the Gospel) in a powerful way.

STEP 11: *Speak gently and seriously*

Silence is of course the "default setting" of the monastic community. To some extent the power of words works on the basis that "less is more": they have more impact if they are carefully chosen and expressive of wisdom. Leaders should not speak loosely or unreflectively. They should never "complain down" — that is, join with those below them in complaining of those above. They should not give way to anger, or at least immoderate anger; if they are angry, their anger should be expressed in a way that will build up rather than destroy. They will likely need to "bare their teeth" on occasion, but they should never forget how a subordinate will feel if reduced to nothing.

STEP 12: *Be aware of how you appear*

Others will take their lead in many ways from leaders — in their appearance, demeanor, feelings. Making an effort to look cheerful and confident (when you might not particularly feel these things at the time) to spread cheerfulness and confidence to others is well-intentioned acting, and appropriate self-awareness in a leader. There is a sacramental quality to leadership, in that leaders should be a sign of God's presence in them and in their work. The abbot's pectoral cross is an obvious example of this sacramentalism, but it should be seen also in his words and actions. There should be integrity between what *is* and what *appears*, and a Benedictine leader must never be a stumbling-block (a *skandalon*) for the faithful, but rather a sign of contradiction to the world's values. Appearances speak, as do words.

BENEDICTINE SCHOOL LEADERSHIP

We have been considering how the picture of the abbot in the Rule of St Benedict can be used as a model for leadership in a very general way, and it is a model that has been applied in a number of contexts, including business and the family.[16] But is a school or college an appropriate parallel to a monastery, and can the leadership of an educational institution really be modeled on an abbot? There are obvious differences. The leadership of employees is different from the leadership of monks or nuns; the relationship between employer and employee is different. More importantly, not all the people in a school are committed to Christ in quite the intentional way of a monastic community. Yet the

16   For instance, in business, see Dollard, Marett-Crosby, and Wright, *Doing Business with Benedict* (London: Continuum, 2002); in the family, see Longenecker, *Listen My Son: St Benedict for Fathers* (Leominster: Gracewing, 2000).

Benedictine model of paternal and benevolent leadership — so well attuned to the needs of human nature — has much to offer the leadership of adults and children in an educational context, as has been discussed above. A leader leads people, and needs to be able to get people to do willingly what they would not necessarily otherwise have done at all. Part of this challenge involves the fact that although the largest group of "stakeholders" in Catholic Benedictine schools will be those who identify themselves as Catholic (including, among others, those who are self-consciously non-practicing and those who are self-consciously orthodox), there will also be other committed or non-practicing Christians, agnostics, and a few atheists. All these have a certain equality as persons and can be reasonably expected to support (at least in a minimal way) the obvious identity and ethos of the Catholic and Benedictine school. But how can the school leader involve everyone, as must the abbot of a monastic community?

Leaders also must have a mission, and in order to lead people in this they must have a vision of how that mission can succeed. There is more chance of a successful mission if the whole team, rather than just part of it, is engaged in its achievement. The success of a Catholic and Benedictine school cannot rest on a minority of committed Catholics on the staff, but will need to involve the whole teaching staff in ongoing formation. Formation (similar to, but distinct from, training) will involve a range of experiences and levels of engagement, depending on the point people consider themselves to be at in their journey, both spiritual and educational. School leaders will need to decide on the minimum level of engagement required, and upon the form and content of formation programs, as appropriate for particular institutions. Formation programs can include seminars on St Benedict and the early history of the Benedictines, on the spirit of Rule, on the meaning of the central virtue of humility, on the history and ethos of a particular monastic community and school, on the particular approach to teaching and learning in that school, and so on. Evening staff formation sessions can also include *lectio divina* and a shared meal, and school leaders should find ways of making such sessions enjoyable rather than an extra burden. Beyond particular formation programs, the following experiences, as they appear from day to day and week to week in the school timetable, can have a formative effect on all staff, and enable a deepening experience of what it means to be a teacher in a Catholic and Benedictine school:

- Initial staff induction (e.g., a new staff induction day)
- Termly in-service training days, always to include something on Benedictine life, rule, education, history, etc.
- Seminars in the Catholic and Benedictine curriculum, Benedictine leadership, etc.
- Readings of the Gospel of the day and from the Rule at weekly staff meetings
- Attending weekly school worship and Sunday Mass
- Attending the Divine Office
- Retreats for new staff—or all staff
- Prayers before meetings
- Reading, study, prayer, communal reflection upon books, articles, and shared resources
- Attending, as middle or senior leaders, meetings of other Benedictine schools
- Assisting with chaplaincy
- Staff *lectio* groups

The students as well as the staff must be involved in the leadership project. If a Benedictine education is truly about transforming lives in Christ, then the students will be those who are to be transformed and then sent out to transform the world. The trajectory of their education is that of the first disciples, whose lives were transformed on hearing the Gospel from the lips of Christ himself when he was personally present to them as a human being; they are taught, they hear, and they are sent out to teach in turn. Of course, this all happens to school students in a very different way from the experience of the first disciples, and in a very different cultural situation. The medium of the evangelization process is the education they receive. Since the Benedictine approach to leadership is built upon an understanding of human nature, and on the wisdom that comes from the study of how and why people act as they do, leadership (in both the theoretical study and the practical experience of it) is part of a Benedictine student's education. Leadership formation involves seeing how the development of creativity and imagination enables the realization of personal vocation, and the vision of the Kingdom that the Gospel makes possible. Benedictine students learn that leadership is service, and however they come to find their vocation (in human fields professional, technical, political, familial, social, or commercial), they *find by doing* that their future life (both work and leisure) is with others, taking responsibility and making good things happen. Leadership becomes central to the discernment of vocation and discipleship. Further, by leading students in leadership teachers also enrich their own experience of leadership and of their own vocation, in a reciprocal and symbiotic process where teachers and students teach and learn from each other.

Where are teachers and students being led in Benedictine education? They are being led towards God, in Christ, and to the fullness of life. If this is to happen, Benedictine school leaders should be conscious that they are doing something radically distinct from those schools which inhabit solely the air of the secular educational world, which has no religious character and may even be hostile to such a thing. All Christian schools are being increasingly brought into a confrontational position with the demands of state bureaucracy as they relate both to the utilitarian content of the school curriculum and to the utilitarian and managerial methods of planning, assessment, and evaluation of that curriculum. Frequently there is a suggestion that anything that cannot be measured has no value. Education becomes instrumentalized, in itself merely a tool, distant from the human heart and the cultivation of wisdom. The compromises and dialogue that often have to happen in the real world can mean the Christian school becomes merely a passive recipient of an alien ideology, neglecting its own traditions and intellectual heritage in favor of what it values in the contemporary world. Christian education needs to be led "out of the box" if it is to become truly transformational. Christian schools must choose to change, or to be changed. The leadership of the school mission is thus a fundamentally spiritual challenge. As one writer has put it: "In the need for a new form of spirituality for church school leadership, it will be important to counter-balance the current emphasis on training, targets, efficiency and competence with an equal emphasis on formation, prayer, vulnerability and confidence."[17]

For the transformational nature of Benedictine education, rooted in the idea and reality of *conversatio,* to work in effective unity with the wider Church, its focus must become the New Evangelization to which Christians have been called by the current and recent popes. The medium of this evangelization, of the post-Christian or part-Christian environment from which most students come, is the Catholic and Benedictine curriculum, which must become increasingly distinctive and conscious of itself as an instrument not of an arid utilitarianism, but of a project to reveal the Gospel message. The second half of this book looks more closely at the shape this learning, curriculum, co-curriculum (the sports, music, drama and other activities outside the classroom), and pastoral care could take.

---

17 John Sullivan, in *Contemporary Catholic Education,* ed. Hayes and Gearon (Leominster: Gracewing, 2002), 102.

CHAPTER 5
Learning

THE FOUR WAYS OF *LECTIO DIVINA*

We saw earlier how central to Benedictine life reading has always been. In the Rule, the balance between time for reading and time for work (or between *otium* and *negotium*) is carefully prescribed, and St Benedict devotes the best hours of the monk's day to reading, and almost as much time to reading as to work. Both work and reading are integrated within the central activity of the monk's life, that is, the *Opus Dei* of the Divine Office, or the Liturgy of the Hours. "There is no Benedictine life without literature,"[1] wrote Jean Leclercq, and it is in grammar (i.e., literature) that we see the essence of Benedictine freedom and Benedictine making, the ordering word of the *logos*. *Lectio divina* is the fertile ground of Benedictine culture, and this *lectio* is, strictly speaking, different in order from other kinds of reading, since it is the prayerful reading of sacred scripture: given the unique subject-matter, and its nature as prayer rather than study, it is entirely *sui generis*.

However, *lectio divina* can be seen as a process similar to other forms of cognition, or re-cognition — the ways we make connection with the reality outside ourselves — and our engagement as human beings with Creation is to be imitative and co-creative. Like all Christian learning, *lectio divina* leads to wisdom and ultimately to God. *Lectio*, then, is not only the ground, or source, but also the template or structure of all Benedictine education. Although the experience of each stage of *lectio divina* happens in time, in a linear way, each stage contains the others; or they may be seen as concentric circles, with reading at the center and

1 Leclercq, 17.

contemplation in the outer circle. We can also list the stages in order of ascent to God, with *lectio* at the bottom, the ground of our activity, and contemplation on the highest rung, as in Guigo's ladder.[2]

Historical perspectives on *lectio divina* are also helpful in showing its connection with, and difference from, secular learning. Patrick Barry points to the emergence of classical learning from the *lectio* of the monasteries: "In the dark time to come in Europe, it was this discipline of *lectio* that led to the emergence of Benedictine monasteries as centers of literacy and learning in scripture and theology. That learning was thorough but never exclusively intellectual, because openness of mind and heart was central to the discipline of *lectio*. This openness led the monasteries in due course to embrace in their study the riches of classical literature and learning."[3] Jean Leclercq distinguishes the reading of Scripture in the cloister from the reading of the (later) school. In the schools, sacred texts came to be studied; in the cloister, they were prayed: "The scholastic *lectio* takes the direction of the *quaestio* and the *disputatio*. The reader puts questions to the text and then questions himself on the subject matter: *quaeri solet*. The monastic *lectio* is oriented toward the *meditatio* and the *oratio*. The objective of the first is science and knowledge; of the second, wisdom and appreciation. In the monastery, the *lectio divina*, which begins with grammar, terminates in compunction, in desire of heaven."[4] A clear distinction can be discerned here between monastic and secular learning, even in the study of Scripture.

Leclercq also reminds us, however, that schools were often part of the monasteries, and he distinguishes two kinds of schools,

2   See Guigo II the Carthusian, *Scala Caeli, or A Ladder of Four Rungs, by Which We May Well Climb to Heaven*.

3   Patrick Barry, OSB, *Saint Benedict's Rule* (Santiago, Chile: Editorial San Juan, 2004), 209.

4   Leclercq, 72.

the monks' schools and the clerical schools. The monks' schools are "internal schools," that is, open to children who are preparing for monastic life and to them alone, or "external" schools to which other children are admitted, and the latter are sometimes located outside the cloister. Cluny, for instance, had an external school in the market town next to the cloister. It was not unusual in such external schools for the teaching to be entrusted to the secular clergy.[5]

These external schools would likely be influenced by the secular clergy's prior education in the liberal arts, and involvement in the active life of their work; the liberal arts in the monastery would have had a function more closely connected to the liturgy and *lectio* of the contemplative life. Yet the difference between a contemplative and an active approach to Christian learning is mostly one of emphasis, action and contemplation being by no means mutually exclusive.

The development of the medieval schools and universities was perhaps rooted in these distinctions between divine and humane reading, such that, as Thomas Merton points out, two distinct approaches to learning diverged: "At the same time, university and monastery tended sometimes to be in very heated conflict, for though they both aimed at 'participation' in and 'experience' of the hidden and the sacred values implanted in the 'ground' and the 'beginning,' they arrived there by different means: the university by *scientia*, intellectual knowledge, and the monastery by *sapientia*, or mystical contemplation."[6] The post-Enlightenment emphasis on *scientia* rather than *sapientia* is one that a modern monastic school (an "external" school in Leclercq's description, run by lay people rather than secular clergy) might challenge. The current state of the culture offers the possibility of a Benedictine moment, when a return to pre-modern notions of learning

5 Ibid., 195.
6 Merton, "Learning to Live," in *Spiritual Master*, 361.

could be fruitfully recovered. The tension between monastery and university, between internal school and external school, will inevitably remain, but insofar as a school attached to a monastery in the modern world cannot but have Christ at its heart, it must consider whether it can with integrity (or *integratedness*) serve uncritically the secular world in the classroom while it is devoted to God in the church. *Lectio divina* may provide a way forward for greater integration. It is important, however, not to confound the two types of *lectio* referred to above, *lectio* as prayer and *lectio* as study (*lectio* as *lesson*). Benedictine schools would want their students to experience *lectio divina* as prayer, and also to experience an education ever more grounded in wisdom.

In the fourfold process of *lectio divina* (*lectio, meditatio, oratio,* and *contemplatio*) we see a movement upwards from text to divine wisdom. It is also interesting to note that we can see a similar upward movement in the process of other medieval academic programs, such as the *trivium* and *quadrivium* of the liberal arts, and in the fourfold structure of exegesis. The language arts of the *trivium* are grammar, dialectic/logic, and rhetoric; the mathematical arts of the *quadrivium* are arithmetic, geometry, music, and astronomy; and the four levels of medieval scriptural exegesis are the literal, the allegorical, the tropological, and the anagogical. *Lectio divina*, the *trivium*, the *quadrivium*, and exegesis are all structures of reading, which map out the way we connect with and deepen our understanding of the text of Creation, so it is not surprising that we can also discern the persons of the Trinity in these structures. All these forms or processes provide means by which the act of reading can lead us to a wisdom based on knowledge, sacred or profane, and some familiarity with these processes can help to reinforce and develop a sense of *lectio divina* as a basis for an authentically Catholic and Benedictine deeper learning, as well as for prayer, and this familiarity may also help to deepen our prayerful experience of *lectio divina* proper.

A BENEDICTINE PEDAGOGY FROM *LECTIO DIVINA*

1. *LECTIO*

The act of reading (a recollection or remembering) corresponds to the grammar (i.e., literature) stage of the *trivium*. It is the basis of all that follows in the liberal arts, and contains the rest. It is the art of letters, which make words and their arrangement, their etymologies and layers of meaning, and the art of the narratives they compose. Familiarity with all the senses of the word *grammar* makes us thoroughly grounded in what is called in exegesis the *literal* level of the text, also called the *historical* (i.e., storytelling) level of the text. We read in this ground, this earth, with humility and attentiveness to the letter. Grammar comes from God the Father, the self-naming, complete I AM.

Guigo calls this stage "feeding," taking in the nourishment that comes from outside us. This stage involves close attention to an object of study, from art (including science) or nature, from the created world or from the world of human artifacts. We *inform* ourselves, registering data, welcoming something into our minds that is not already there, and this involves turning to the content or material of the lesson. The "text," if not Scripture, is still capable (even if only in a negative sense) of revealing the beauty, truth, or goodness of the world; a study of evil, Shakespeare's *Macbeth* for example, will serve to illustrate the good, through the guidance of good teaching. The text is life-giving food, and we remember the saying in scripture, "What father when his son asks for bread gives him a stone?" This should put an emphasis on quality, since not all texts are equally worthy of study, and the text should be suited to the capacities of the students while challenging them to begin the journey that *lectio divina* represents. The teacher asks, "How does the text chosen make for wisdom, the intellectual and spiritual formation of the pupil?" The "text" might be literary, historical, empirical data, a work of art — anything which in itself is potentially revelatory of God working through his creation or the work of human hands. The teacher will give room for the text to make its impressions on the minds of the pupils without his close intervention at this stage, and the text is beginning to become a threshold, a bridge, a crossing-point between the teacher and the pupil, the "father" and the "son."

2. MEDITATIO

The act of reflection on what is read corresponds to the dialectic/logic stage of the *trivium* and the *allegorical* level of exegesis. There is a movement away, outwards from the literal level of the text into what it also conveys, by analogy: in exegesis, this anticipates, includes, and prepares for the next two levels. Dialectic is the stage of thinking, arguing, articulating possibilities; it is a stage full of energy, and moves powerfully like water. This is the stage of the Son, the mediator, the Logos, the middle between earth and heaven.

Guigo calls this stage "chewing." A *kenosis* is involved here, emptying the mind of its preconceptions, just as chewing is preparing food for movement into the stomach. Reflection might involve annotation of the text, a stage of interactivity between learner and text. The pupil reflects on his own, or in pairs or groups. Reasoning begins to happen, and a kindling of fire in the mind and heart. The matter is taken (through taste) into the hearts of the pupils, pondered (weighed) there, or ruminated upon, as food in a stomach. *Information* turns into *knowledge*, and the significance of the knowledge of the heart, rather than of the mind, is important here: the whole person is *thinking*, in a kind of thinking which goes beyond analytical criticism (cf. Wordsworth, "We murder to dissect") or mere cleverness. A mirroring is also happening here — of self, of pupils (by the teacher), of the world around us. The pupil sees himself mirrored in the teacher and in the world around him. This is what Einstein seems to be referring to in this observation: "the state of mind which enables a [person] to do work of this kind [mathematics] is akin to that of the religious worshipper or the lover; the daily effort comes from no deliberate intention or program, but straight from the heart." Elsewhere Einstein wrote, "The most beautiful experience we can have is the mysterious. It is the fundamental emotion which stands at the cradle of true art and true science.... I am satisfied with the mystery of the eternity of life and a glimpse of the marvelous structure of the existing world, together with the devoted striving to comprehend a portion ... of the Reason that manifests itself in nature."[7]

3. *ORATIO*

The act of reception (of "taking in"), like prayer, corresponds to speaking, utterance, or written verbal expression, which is, in the *trivium*, rhetoric. (In a sense, prayer is the highest form of rhetoric.) This is a stage of transformation, of making new wholes, a mimesis in which we speak like God, in the Spirit who prays in us and for us. This is the Spirit who came in the form of tongues of fire, and who brings the gift of tongues. This stage corresponds to the *tropological* (the moral — in human terms, a remaking) stage in exegesis, the turning (*trope*) inwards.

Guigo calls this stage "savoring." An I-thou relationship has formed; the pupil is conscious of being a subject with another subject, not a subject confronted by an object, in a sensing that reality is personal. The heart of the pupil gives voice in oral or written response, and there is an affirmation, joy, or *understanding*, in the sense of *comprehendere*, which also suggests a comparison, as in the metaphors of the psalms, connections being made between one thing and another in light of the unity of all things. The moment of conception happens, conception as in a *conceit* or *concept*. The pupil is fully open to the other, and a kind of *metanoia* has occurred, the heart has been broken open. There is speech and expression based on the experience of the subject, and a co-creative response occurs. At its deepest level, such learning may happen only once or twice in a human lifetime; at a less deep level, it is happening in moments of real, even joyful insight.

4. *CONTEMPLATIO*

The transformative act of contemplative seeing happens in the heaven that is within us. This is the *anagogical* (spiritual or

7   Quoted in Lichtmann, 81.

mystical) level of exegesis, and corresponds to the direct vision of the triune God. At this stage, perhaps, the earthy and earthly *trivium* changes into the *quadrivium*, the heavenly arts of number and proportion (arithmetic, geometry, music, and astronomy). This is a place of air, or perhaps (as the pre-Socratics suggested) of the *quintessence* (the fifth element), the aether, which might also be a kind of fire, but in any case is a *locus refrigerii, lucis et pacis.*

Guigo calls this stage "digesting," implying a certain repose. The heart is at rest to be remade in the vision of the thing seen, which is the beginning of *wisdom*, humility, seeing the *reason* of the universe. The ladder of ascent is of course also the way of humility, and there is formation in the mind of the image of truth, beauty, and goodness. This learning remakes the pupil in the moment of vision. As Jan van Ruysbroeck put it, "We become what we behold; we behold what we are."[8] The classroom can now be seen as a *templum*, a space of vision. This is also the moment of birth; to quote Meister Eckhart, "When the Son is born in the soul, God shines out of every creature."[9] The teacher is the midwife to the birth, which is also the moment of the death of old ideas, in a new "realization." There is a moment of access, a breaking-through.

As Aquinas said, all learning is a process of *tradere contemplativa,* sharing the fruits of contemplation.

Not every lesson will bring a close realization of the ideal, but unless we have an idea of what we are aiming for, we'll not achieve it at all, and something else, something even alien, will become our rationale.

HALLMARKS OF A LESSON IN A BENEDICTINE CLASSROOM

Let us return to the ABCU's "Ten Hallmarks of Benedictine Education." What follows is an attempt to consider whether we can discern within the Benedictine tradition of learning a specifically Benedictine pedagogy, such that we might speak meaningfully of

8 Ibid., 110.
9 Ibid.

a *style* of teaching and learning, in relation to Catholic truth in a Benedictine setting.

Rather than looking merely to "attach" a perspective on our lessons that refers to "ethos," we might look more radically to define new parameters to shape our lessons, other than those that refer, in a content- and value-free way, to school inspection regimes, or other generic sets of lesson observation criteria, useful though they may be. In doing so, we need not jettison entirely these other models, but we will certainly deepen them, prove their mettle, and integrate what they hold of value into the "Benedictine wisdom tradition"[10] of which the ABCU document speaks.

If these new parameters are of use in developing a Catholic and Benedictine curriculum, then further thinking on the specifics in the classroom, at the "chalk face" of the school, should be integrated with them. They could fruitfully be seen to inspire the form and content of lessons and activities across the curriculum and co-curriculum, just as they apply to all aspects of life in a Benedictine learning community.

1. *LOVE is seen in* A STRIVING FOR THE OTHER'S GOOD

Love is simply, and in unqualified terms, Love, proceeding directly from the center of the school, which is Christ in God. In a lesson, this is seen in the teacher's love for his or her pupils, the basis of all else that happens. The teacher's love is the eager, active desire for the pupils' good, their healthy growth in mind and heart, their achievement and creativity. The teacher wants what is best for them, which is for them to be the best they can be. Love is also seen in the teacher's love for the subject, for the aspects of creation that it demonstrates, and for the beauty, truth, and goodness that it allows us to see. The teacher's love informs his language, manner, actions, and self-sacrifice. The love of learning is bound up with the desire for God, and makes joy a characteristic

---

10   ABCU, "Education within the Benedictine Wisdom Tradition." https://www.abcu.info/index.asp?SEC=94EFD1ED-B758-49CE-A3EA-1688AFF-C9AC7&DE=47641124-0236-45D2-9FD4-2B0617CC3C1A.

note of the lesson in a Benedictine school. The joy and the delight experienced are a foretaste of heaven. While laughter may be rare, smiles will be frequent, affirming of the joy in what is being seen and experienced in the lesson. Love leads the teacher to see the class as individual persons, and with skill the teacher is able to differentiate the teaching and accommodate it to the nature of each particular pupil, remembering that they are all members of a classroom learning community.

2. PRAYER *is seen in* ATTENTIVENESS

The prayerfulness of reading is central to Benedictine activity, in the choir, the study, and the classroom. The text is the word, which represents the Word, or God's self-expression in creation. We attend to some object of inquiry, or contemplation, through which we find what helps us to grow. Even in texts that are not divine in origin, language reveals the knowledge of creation and contributes to wisdom, the grounding of the soul in God. As we have seen above, a lesson of a Benedictine character will typically have some act of reading at its center, and the quality of the "text" (or object) will be such that it cultivates a developed use of language in the soul of the student. The content or matter of the lesson will be such that it can reveal the good, the true, and the beautiful in works or objects in nature and art. Nature (or creation) is itself a text written in the language of the divine Logos. Learning activities which are not "academic" will also involve some kind of turning to an object outside the self, in God or his creation, which is a referent through which we raise our hearts and minds to him. A prayerful attentiveness, in silence, quiet, or calm, with focus and concentration, pervades any Benedictine activity. Prayer itself might come into the lesson, at the beginning or end, in the Angelus, or in times of silence, promoted perhaps by images on the walls of the classroom.

3. STABILITY *is seen in* CONSISTENCY

The class community is rooted in its place in space and time, each lesson part of a larger scheme of work, all lessons having a consistency of character, in an excellence determined by a higher order than the school inspection criteria, which the lesson fulfills yet transcends. The lesson reveals commitment to constantly reiterated objectives, to a project of inquiry or learning, which continues through the course of the year (or two years), and then beyond. There is also commitment in the teacher to the pupils, in the pupils to their teacher, in the pupils to each other. The profession of the teacher is not a job that begins and ends with the lesson, however well-crafted a piece of teaching art that lesson may be. Teaching is a vocation, frequently (if not usually) a lifelong occupation for the person called to it as a state of life. It is a vocation that forms the teacher as well as the pupil. In a Benedictine school, particularly a residential one, as in other schools that are central to the life of a particular place, it is common for teachers to teach more than one member or even generation of the same family, and this continuity in relationship is an extension of the fact of relationship that exists in each classroom. Pupils in a Benedictine school value their teacher as one with whom they have a personal relationship, perhaps for life — even into eternal life — and in order that they might learn how to live.

4. CONVERSATIO MORUM *is seen in* TRANSFORMATION

Conversatio leads us to see learning as transformative of the lives of those who participate in it. When a lesson happens to work at the deepest possible level, it can contain a life-changing experience, which might be a moment of insight or of grace, which radically reorients the future direction of the learner (or the teacher). Such moments cannot be determined by the teacher, but the teacher can so dispose the materials and the activities that such moments, whether profound or less profound, are more likely to occur. Learning is a lifelong process of growth towards wisdom and God rather the mere manipulation of data: it concerns transformation, not information; a continuing way that ends in eternal life, rather than simply a destination to exam success. Teaching and learning thus essentially constitute a spiritual process in which information about and knowledge of the world around us are steps in a way to wisdom. Wisdom cannot grow without a certain degree of information and knowledge (of which it will sometimes include a great deal), but it is of a higher order, and implies the spiritual wholeness of which even knowledge is only a part. The student is being continually welcomed into a way of life which provides resources to which he can return again and again throughout his life. In speaking, as we often do, of formation of pupils and teachers in Catholic schools, we understand this as *formation towards transformation*.

5. OBEDIENCE *is seen in* LISTENING

The Benedictine student is characteristically a good listener, and so is a Benedictine teacher. The mutual obedience that St. Benedict enjoins in his Rule is seen in a Benedictine classroom. There is dialogue rather than monologue, and the teacher is a conversationalist of a high order; he or she knows when to stop talking. In speaking, he is careful to use language with respect—a respect for language itself and a due respect for the age and sensibilities of his pupils—and the pupils imitate this in the teacher, from whom they take their lead. The Socratic method of crafted dialogue is particularly well-suited to the Benedictine lesson, the pupils finding the "answer" in themselves through the skillful drawing-out by the teacher. They find and develop their own capacities to learn without the teacher being present, and yet they hear the voice of the teacher in their mind even when he is not present. (They may continue to hear the voice of the teacher at different times throughout their lives, and they may learn from the teacher how to recognize the voice of Christ in their hearts.) The pupils are obedient without consciousness of being so; disobedience has not occurred to them, because their minds have been successfully focused on the object outside themselves, and to which they attend. They listen carefully to the other voices in the classroom, voices that come from the texts they read, or the voices they hear from the digital projector or audio recording. Listening—or obedience—is an act not so much of submission as of engagement, not passive but active.

6. DISCIPLINE *is seen in* DECORUM

The ordering of the Benedictine lesson does not rely in the first place on the external imposition of discipline, for example, in the form of rewards and sanctions, because the motive towards order lies in the attraction of the tasks, the wonder that is being unfolded, the sense of being drawn by something and someone worth following. Each pupil is seen as capable of wisdom, and so the teacher does not rest in continuing to lead the pupils farther and farther along the path of learning, as it becomes at some times broader and at others deeper. The gifted and talented (all the pupils in different ways) have their gifts and talents further exercised; those with special learning needs (again, all of us to some extent) have accommodation made; the whole flock is cared for by the good shepherd or teacher. There is a right way to behave in the classroom, because it is a *templum*, a time and a space that provides a prospect of the world outside us, a prospect that can lead to heaven. The lesson in the classroom is a kind of liturgy in a kind of oratory (in the sense of a place of prayer), and so behavior that disposes us to hear and see God is appropriate and necessary. There is no underestimation of the capacities of students, since this takes an inappropriate possession of the student and the learning process, which should be allowed to depend on the Spirit. The self-discipline of the teacher, as an example of both teacher and learner, informs the character and so the behavior of the pupil.

7. HUMILITY *is seen in* WISDOM

As we have seen, for St. Benedict, the search for humility is the search for wisdom. Freed from the modern privileging of knowledge over wisdom, the Benedictine teacher is not afraid to say that he doesn't know, that he is on the same way as his pupil. He knows that the pupil has his own knowledge of valuable things. At the same time, the teacher speaks freely of what he does know, without self-consciousness or trying to appear more knowledgeable than he is. The teacher appreciates the integration of all knowledge, from theology at one end of the spectrum to the crafts at the other, and he is grounded in understanding that the knowledge of the things of the world around us is a form of celebration, and appreciation, of the created order that God saw as good, since it reflects Him. While the teacher rejoices in the success of his students, he knows that learning is not truly about their self-promotion, or future economic success, or pride in being better than others, but in their learning how to make use of knowledge to become of service to others. Benedictine learning is about finding the humility, the wisdom that allows us to become fully human in Christ.

8. STEWARDSHIP *is seen in* RESPECT

Teachers are stewards of what and whom they have in their care, their subject and their pupils. They have to give an account of that which has been entrusted to them by the Lord when he comes to reclaim what is his. They recognize their work, their pupils, and their calling as gifts held in trust. The act of teaching is an act of conservation of the natural and built environments, the cultural, aesthetic, and moral milieu in which the school finds itself. Teachers do not hold their subject or their pupils in possession; all belongs to God, as a window (or a mirror) onto Him, who cannot yet be seen face-to-face. The lesson will reveal the mutual respect of pupil and teacher, and the respect the teacher has for his or her subject, his material, and his calling. It will engender a respect for the things of nature and art (including science) that reveal the wonder, mystery, beauty, truth, and goodness of the world that God has made in Christ. Respect implies turning outward from ourselves to the object of study, that is, the world around us, and seeing its infinite value, however much it has fallen. This understanding of the difference between the world as God intends it and the world as it is defaced by sin leads the student and teacher to consider how their lifelong work can help to build up the Kingdom of God. The ordering of the classroom, its furnishing and decoration, and the way that energy and materials are used there but not wasted all engender a spirit of gratitude and enjoyment. The environment of the classroom is integrated sensitively with the subject-matter of the lessons, avoiding anything extraneous, and yet reflecting the nature of the classroom as a kind of home.

9. *HOSPITALITY* is seen in OPENNESS

The Benedictine classroom is an open space, and one which welcomes pupils and visitors, including other teachers who conduct observation as a kind of visitation, in the sense of inspection. The teacher is not closed off from the scrutiny that he conducts of his pupils. He is open to creativity and to ideas, to all regardless of age, sex, class, creed, culture, or color; his classroom is a place where all are greeted as Christ. The lesson enables the opening of minds to God, to knowledge of his world, and to the way of perfection. The relationship of the teacher and pupil is like that of host and guest in the mutuality of obligation and courtesy, in the building of communion in the classroom as a kind of home, a place of peace as well as of work and prayer. Intellectually speaking, in the Benedictine lesson there is openness to whatever there is in the beauty, truth, or goodness of the subject-matter, because Christ is seen in these things, and Christ is welcomed wherever his face is seen. Both pupil and teacher feel "at home" in the classroom, and in the lesson, because humane learning — learning for humanity — is present there. Pupils in a Benedictine lesson become secure enough to grow securely and develop as learners.

10. *COMMUNITY* is seen in COOPERATION

In a Benedictine lesson, it is evident that pupils are not patients who undergo, or suffer, the administrations of the teacher, as if they were Mr Gradgrind's inclined plane of empty, atomized vessels waiting to be filled, as in an image of modern, industrialized education.[11] Benedictine work is essentially cooperative. In the *Opus Dei* of the Divine Office, all the monks contribute to the liturgical action. The teacher and the pupil cooperate in the learning process, which will include cooperation and mutual support among pupils, such that they can see each other as teachers as well as learners. To teach is a common human activity before it is vocational and professional. All parents, for example, are teachers. Cooperation involves the dialogue that is characteristic of the

---

11   See Charles Dickens, *Hard Times*, Chapter 1.

essential community of teacher and pupil, master and disciple. In the community of the classroom, the pupil learns how to build community in the wider world, through dialogue and mutual care.

A TRANSCENDENTAL EDUCATION

How are we, then, to summarize the Benedictine pedagogical approach, if it is not simply to be "education by Benedictine monastics" or a certain kind of monastic "atmosphere"? The documents of a Benedictine educational colloquium, held at the Abbey of Maredsous in 1981, put it thus:

> The Rule of St Benedict stresses quite a series of aspects which have a pedagogical value. Here are a few of them:
>
> 1. The balance that has to be discovered between the principle of authority and the respect of the liberty of the individual.
> 2. The synthesis between the reality of the community and the personal life of each individual. In other words it could be said that the Rule recommends a community-personalism.
> 3. The Benedictine Rule endeavors to find a balance between manual and intellectual work, between thought and meditation.
> 4. For Saint Benedict, there is a refusal to let oneself be locked in the classic opposition between things profane and sacred. For the author of the Benedictine Rule everything is sacred, which means that everything conveys a message of symbols and meaning.[12]

The Benedictine school therefore is marked by:

---

12 *Benedictini Vivendi Praeceptores: Actes du Colloque de Pédagogie bénédictine* (Denée, Belgium: Editions de Maredsous, 1981), 105–6.

1. The importance given to a person-to-person relationship of the adult and the youngster in a climate of realistic trust.

2. The care of improving the whole human person according to his different potentialities.

3. The sensibility to values of "discretion," wisdom, balance, peace, beauty and joy.

4. The respect of nature and of the environment. This respect for nature harmonizes also with the respect of "time" which implies the virtue of patience.

5. The Benedictine education is also characterized by openness to the Absolute, the God revealed in Christ, to the sense of what is essential.[13]

The documents make the point that the distinctiveness of a Benedictine pedagogy lies particularly in ethos rather than in a method or a *ratio studiorum*, but we have argued above that *lectio divina* offers the possibility of a more defined methodological pedagogy than the delegates of the Maredsous colloquium necessarily envisaged. This arises out of a more deliberate attempt to describe (rather than define) a Benedictine approach to learning that will meet the cultural needs of Western society, and possibly the needs of other parts of the world where the Benedictine Rule is followed and the modern Western cultural influence is felt. The educational need in our culture at present is for a deep learning, and if this is to be passed on in a Benedictine context, it will need teachers (many if not most of them lay) consciously formed in the Benedictine tradition. Such formation will not take place simply by osmosis, but will need the kind of preparation discussed above in Chapter 4.

The Benedictine classroom, the relationship between teacher and pupil, and the whole education itself together form a crossing-place of transformation. This is transfiguring, and transcendental, because it opens the student to the vision of Christ

13   Ibid., 106.

in the world, and the signs of God's presence in the qualities of goodness, truth, and beauty. In the next chapter, we consider in more detail how this Catholic curriculum of goodness, truth, and beauty can be understood and followed in the Benedictine tradition. The content of the curriculum in a Benedictine school will not be distinct from the nature of the curriculum in any Catholic school, except insofar as it will find many examples from the Benedictine tradition as well as from the wider Church. This Catholic curriculum must also be carefully and consciously considered if it is to meet the cultural needs of our time.

CHAPTER 6

Curriculum

A CATHOLIC CURRICULUM

There have been various attempts to reassess the curriculum of the Catholic school, college, or university as Catholic teachers aim to meet the needs of the Church and the world in particular times. Certain models endure, as they are passed on within certain traditions and institutions, where they come to occupy privileged positions. It becomes possible, therefore, to speak of Catholic *curricula* as different responses to the question of what makes the content and methods of a Catholic education distinctive. For some, a Catholic curriculum is essentially a medieval curriculum, grounded in the seven liberal arts. Arising out of this, the classical curriculum grounded in Latin and Greek, the staple of the English grammar and public schools, fits neatly into Catholic versions of these models and comes to be seen as authentically Catholic, even when it is simply classical. The pervasive influence of Jesuit education brought with it the coherence of the *ratio studiorum*, and the Ignatian model is seen by some to exemplify best the Catholic curriculum. In modernity, the re-articulation of liberal education and the idea of the gentleman by John Henry Newman, redefined against the alternative of Victorian utilitarianism, continues to be a major inspiration into postmodernity, even among those who don't agree with Newman's stance.[1] The Catholic curriculum can also be conceived as a version of a modern model such as the International Baccalaureate (IB) with a Catholic theory of knowledge, or of

---

1   See Stefan Collini, *What Are Universities For?* (London: Penguin, 2012). Collini gives respectful treatment to Newman, even when he doesn't agree with him, and he recognizes that Newman's vision is still important.

vocation, filling the God-shaped hole in what is otherwise a broad and balanced selection of subjects.

Yet the specifically confessional understanding of a Catholic education, rooted in catechesis, religious studies and shared liturgy, prayer and sacraments, with the subjects studied in the classroom being very much secondary to the religious life of the school, persists.[2] Others suggest that the rich heritage of Catholic social teaching is what makes the Catholic school distinctive and true to itself.[3] But whatever the particular subjects studied, the end of the Catholic curriculum is formation of the young in those inner directions that make for "the human person: with his openness to truth and beauty, his sense of moral goodness, his freedom and the voice of his conscience, with his longings for the infinite and for happiness, man questions himself about God's existence. In all this he discerns signs of his spiritual soul. The soul, the 'seed of eternity we bear in ourselves, irreducible to the merely material,' can have its origin only in God."[4]

If, then, we consider that the Catholic curriculum is made up of a number of possible subjects and classroom-based activities, we shall see that different Catholic schools have always answered for themselves the question of what courses of study should be followed, to meet the needs of pupils, the Church, and the world at different times and in different places. Independent Benedictine houses and their schools particularly exemplify a diversity of possible responses. But this is not to say that any one Catholic school's curriculum is as good as another's. It may be seen that in a particular Catholic school there is little to distinguish its classroom from that of the secular school down the road, except the presence of the crucifix on the wall. In order to

2   See Sean Whittle, *A Theory of Catholic Education* (London: Bloomsbury, 2015). Whittle provides a thoughtful critique of the confessional position, and suggests an alternative based in his reading of Karl Rahner.

3   See Gerald Grace, "Catholic social teaching should permeate the Catholic secondary school curriculum: an agenda for reform," in *International Studies in Catholic Education* 5, no. 1 (March 2013): 99–109.

4   *The Catechism of the Catholic Church*, Part 1, Section 1, Chapter 1, ii, S33. http://www.vatican.va/archive/ENG0015/_PA.HTM.

survive, in either a state-maintained or an independent sector, a Catholic school may in reality be driven much more by state requirements on the one hand or by a sense of what the market dictates on the other: religion might be downplayed for fear of antagonizing either the commissar or the commercialist. But in a Catholic school which has resolved to treat its religion as much more than so much gloss, the question must be faced: what are we called to be and do *now*, at this cultural moment, within our own particular Catholic tradition and in our own particular mission territory? In their discernment of the signs of the times, recent popes have called the Church to a "New Evangelization," the evangelization of the formerly Christian. If post-Christian man is locked in himself by the secular materialistic worldview then there is only a culture of death; if man is entire of himself, he loses his humanity, sunk in the deepest poverty. In such a cultural climate, the Catholic school must work out an understanding of itself as a place of pre-evangelization, a readying of the ground to receive the Gospel of Life: "This would be focused on how the Catholic school tailors its educational distinctiveness to meet the needs of those who are open to wider questions about God and human existence yet are not ready to respond to the call of faith. Parents who choose to send their children to a Catholic school should be aware that there is a distinctive anthropology underpinning its curriculum and pedagogy."[5] If a relativistic approach to the curriculum in a Catholic school is to be avoided, this then is a central test: does it reflect a Christian understanding of the nature of man and his place in creation?

The Benedictine motto, *ut in omnibus glorificetur Deus* — "that God in all things may be glorified" — might serve as a guiding principle to the integrated, coherent, and appropriate Catholic curriculum. The phrase comes from Chapter 57 of the Rule, "The Artisans of the Monastery," and it symbolizes the central importance of humility in St Benedict's model of the evangelized life:

---

5 Ronnie Convery, Leonardo Franchi, and Raymond McCluskey, *Reclaiming the Piazza: Catholic Education as a Cultural Project* (Leominster: Gracewing, 2014), 7.

"The evil of avarice must have no part in establishing prices, which
should, therefore, always be a little lower than people outside the
monastery are able to set, *so that in all things God may be glorified*
[1 Peter 4:11]." On one level, this is a modest, practical statement
about price control in local markets — leading perhaps to a sustainable, steady, and moderate income for the monastery, but
also perhaps to its opposite, where a larger business operation
undercuts local traders with their more limited scale of production: as such, the basis of an interesting Business and Economics
lesson in a Benedictine classroom. But against the "dismal science" of economics sits this jewel from scripture, reminding us
that the sacred becomes manifest in the human, and the Gospel
of joy shines in dark and dull places. In all places, in all subjects,
the purpose of the Catholic curriculum is to reveal God in the
world, for "whatever discloses the human, discloses the divine."[6]
Such revelation, or disclosure, will undoubtedly be achieved
through ethos and method — the way of teaching in a Catholic
school — but it should also be done by sharing the considerable
Catholic resources of theology, literature, poetry, science, art, and
music, among other subjects; to ignore this inheritance would
be to ignore the Catholic "fruits of contemplation" that show
in practice what a Christian understanding of the world looks
like. But the predisposition to share the fruits of Catholic learning and culture does not mean the exclusion of non-Catholic
or non-Christian works, writers, and thinkers. That which truly
reveals the truly human also reveals the divine.

Of course, not all that has been made by Catholics is of great
cultural value; to put the matter another way, it is not the Catholic vision alone that gives a cultural artifact its artistic, scientific,
or literary value. But it is easily demonstrated that some of the
very best that has been thought and said is made out of a Catholic
vision of reality — *because* it is Catholic and not *in spite of* this,
contrary to the dominant cultural perspective nowadays. Insofar

---

6   David Albert Jones and Stephen Barrie, *Thinking Christian Ethos: The
Meaning of Catholic Education* (London: Catholic Truth Society, 2015), 108.

as Catholic schools facilitate the secular culture rather than challenge it, they will adopt utilitarian approaches to course content, especially if they work according to state-prescribed syllabi and examination specifications. If the ends of the course are most importantly to achieve the highest exam results, then course content will be determined by relative simplicity, "relevance" to the pupils' immediate concerns, superficial connections with the supposed tastes of the young, and all sorts of perspectives designed to require less and less of the pupil and the teacher. But if the ends of the course are transfigured by the transcendental vision, then inevitably the choice of materials, tests, and tasks will be affected. Here, the Catholic curriculum will certainly be counter-cultural, because a Catholic understanding of the nature of the human will mean a different view of art, literature, science, music, and the rest than prevails within the secular culture and the educational establishment that emerges from it. As Chesterton said of the late nineteenth-century nihilism in Ibsen, "The human race, according to religion, fell once, and in falling gained knowledge of good and evil. Now we have fallen a second time, and only the knowledge of evil remains to us."[7] Can we be confident that if the young study only the products of the dominant post-Christian culture they will achieve a knowledge of the Good any more than of the True and the Beautiful?

Catholic schools are, as Gerald Grace has pointed out, prone to "mission drift."[8] It is helpful, therefore, for schools periodically to review their statement of mission or vision, or any other guiding articulation of what they believe they are to do. Mission statements, as a prose form, have come into educational institutions from the world of business and commerce, but the sense of "mission" is ultimately derived from religion. In this sense, mission statements should not be seen as wholly alien strategic devices. The challenges in composing meaningful statements are,

7 G. K. Chesterton, *Heretics* (London: Bodley Head, 1905), 32.
8 Gerald Grace, *Faith, Mission and Challenge in Catholic Education* (Abingdon, Oxon: Routledge, 2017), 167.

however, manifold: how to avoid cliché and generic language; how
to be brief and pithy without being reductive; how to be clear
and coherent in the midst of consultation and review. A single
sentence is a helpful limit, as in this mission statement recently
composed in a Benedictine school:

> [This school]
> welcomes its pupils
> into a Christ-centered education
> in goodness, truth and beauty,
> to form them in humility
> for service and leadership
> in a changing world.

This is Benedictine Catholic education in a nutshell, or, perhaps,
a mustard seed. A certain trajectory shapes the statement: pupils
come in, they experience for a time this education, and they
go out to live the rest of their lives. The Catholic curriculum is
expressed in the transcendentals of Goodness, Truth, and Beauty.
The Benedictine ethos is expressed in the welcoming that is
essential for every pupil; this education, while being formative,
is not coercive or objectifying, as the pupils are subjects in a
world of other subjects. The education is Christ-centered (rather
than being child- or teacher-centered), since as Benedict puts
it we "prefer nothing to Christ." The means, method, or pedagogy is expressed in "humility" of both pupil and teacher on the
sure-footed path to wisdom; the purpose is at once "service" and
"leadership," understood in Benedictine terms as being closely
identified. It is accurate on many levels to speak of the "changing
world," yet this also hints at the importance of *conversatio morum*;
a Benedictine education is for the rest of one's life, a continuing
disposition of growth in and towards Christ.

GOODNESS

A Catholic curriculum designed to reveal the attributes of God reflects the duty of the Church "to foster and elevate all that is found to be true, good and beautiful in the human community."[9] In reflecting God himself, these transcendentals also reflect natural human inclinations to feel, to think, and to want. The transcendentals include each other, since fundamentally they are, like God, *one*. Parents want their children to be successful at school, but more than this they want their children to be happy; deeper still they want their children to be good persons, and whether the parents are Catholics or not they recognize that a Catholic school will help their children to be good. The essence of Western education is in the Greek *arête* and *paideia*: the training of the young in the ways of virtue, as this has been understood in classical and then Christian terms. "Only God is good," Jesus reminds us, pointing to the source of all good in the Father, who wills the good for his children, who in turn, like the rest of Creation, are seen by the Father as good. Parents share in this fatherhood of God as they desire that their children be good. Goodness is found in the fulfillment of their nature, in being good in relation to themselves, to others, and to God. The wider culture is apt to understand goodness in Rousseauist terms, as something given by nature and only spoiled by subsequent interference by education and religion. But the Church knows that natural goodness is mixed with the consequences of the Fall, so virtue must be habituated and consciously pursued. The good is not always obvious, and nothing can be assumed in a world of multifarious and frequently antithetical cultural influences.

Pupils will experience different occasions in the classroom on which questions arise of good and evil, right and wrong, justice and unfairness. Nowadays, such questions occur in relation to prevalent ideas about "equality" and "access," as well as to the welfare of pupils themselves and of others. If secular ideas of

---

9 *Gaudium et Spes*, § 76. http://www.vatican.va/archive/hist_councils/ ii_vatican_council/documents/vat-ii_const_19651207_gaudium-et-spes_en.html.

what constitutes the good for both individuals and society are not simply to be passively accepted and propagated, then the Catholic school will need to address questions of the good from the perspective of the Catholic faith. In revealing the nature of goodness to pupils, theology will be a core subject for all pupils. Christian ethics can be formally studied, to become habituated in the context of friendship — in its widest, Aristotelian sense — and in the context of an understanding of human relationships. In this respect, the study of the humanities is crucial, and most young people will find the study of ethics more accessible in the experience of literature than in the more abstract terms of theology. What makes a "good" character, in a play or a novel, worthy of the description? Ideas of the good will be considered within possible human situations that allow pupils to consider what is *humane* and what is *inhumane*, what makes for human flourishing in love, and what limits or stifles human growth. Such considerations of right and wrong will come into the study of other subjects, too: psychology and economics, history and philosophy. It is important that the study of the Good become a part not only of the theology curriculum, but of all subjects that encompass the thoughts and actions of human beings; the alternative would be to "ghettoize" the Catholic curriculum in the theology department. Apart from the fact that this would not make for an integrated and coherent Catholic curriculum, it would not meet the needs of all pupils, since not all pupils respond in the same way or at the same time; at certain times, theology *per se* will not appeal to them.

To some extent, attention to *values* has in recent times predominated over attention to *virtues*. Catholic schools have variously referred to "Gospel values," and we have seen above that Benedictine educational institutions have variously articulated the human qualities or "good things" that they hold to be fruitful in building up both individuals and community. In Britain, there has been a state-sponsored attempt to enshrine "fundamental British values" in schools.[10] But as David Albert Jones has argued,

---

10   "Democracy, the rule of law, individual liberty and mutual respect for

rather than speaking in a vague way of "values" that we support, we need to identify whether these named values are best understood as virtues, and, if so, where virtue lies. What are the various goods that need to be integrated by the virtues? How can we identify what is good, reasonable, right and just in particular cases? The virtues need to be integrated in the life of each person, thus education should seek the *integral formation of the person*, the simultaneous formation of the different aspects of a good character (the virtues) so that they comprise a well-integrated unity.[11]

In an important sense, it is virtues rather than values that make things happen, especially if the virtues are articulated as adverbs rather than the more usual nouns: what is it, for instance, to act humbly, courageously, or justly? Furthermore, without the wider context of religious faith, values are apt to become ends in themselves, rather in the way that "tolerance" is usually seen as an unqualified good, even when the most tolerant of people will always have things, persons, or views that they will not tolerate. A culture of "values" can lead to a "virtues-lite" approach, even in Catholic schools, which consciously or unconsciously adopt (or adapt to) the prevailing secular culture, such as that of Western liberal democracy. Catholic values can easily be distorted to resemble a version of liberal values, but they are not the same thing. And when Catholic religious education moves away (often for very good reasons) from a traditional, catechetical approach to formation, then the cardinal virtues of temperance, prudence, fortitude, and justice and the theological virtues of faith, hope, and charity can be sidelined.

Nothing about pupils' prior doctrinal knowledge can be assumed in the Catholic school today. Even in the rare cases where

---

and tolerance of those with different faiths and beliefs." https://assets.publishing.service.gov.uk/government/uploads/system/uploads/attachment_data/file/380595/SMSC_Guidance_Maintained_Schools.pdf.

11   Jones and Barrie, 31.

a pupil's spiritual and religious formation has been sustained in family and parish, notions of what constitutes the good person, the good life, or the good society will likely be informed more by the general notions of the culture than by Church teaching. The nature of the human being is no longer reflected in enduring societal norms relating to sexuality, marriage, family, the beginning and end of human life, and the way that technology and medicine interconnect with human physiology. "Gospel values" such as compassion, tolerance, and mercy are put at the service of "choice," so that conclusions can be reached that are very much at variance with Catholic teaching. It is in this cultural milieu that the young meet ethical questions with regard to homosexual unions, divorce and remarriage, abortion, euthanasia, and transgender rights; where the state allows or, indeed, promotes "rights" with regard to such matters, in opposing them the Church seems behind the times, irrelevant, and (hypocritically) contradictory of "Gospel values." In the arena of politics and society, again, political systems grounded in a Marxist analysis of the nature of human society can often seem to the young to be more Christian than traditional Catholic teaching in support of the family as the basic unit of society, the place of freedom in the operation of markets, and the limits of the state. Only an ethical education grounded in the virtues and referred to accounts of how human beings behave in the fields of economics and business, politics and history, will help the young to develop a critique of the *Zeitgeist* rather than unthinkingly to accept it. A study of Catholic Social Teaching and what it has to say about the "common good" should be accommodated wherever possible in the classroom, and Catholic bioethics be brought to bear on questions that arise not only in the theology classroom but also in biology and pre-med classes.

Study itself is an exercise in virtue, as are the other activities that pupils undertake in school. The "school for the Lord's service" is a *gymnasium* in both the older and the newer senses, a place in which the young exercise not only physical and intellectual faculties but also the moral faculty that allows them to persist in difficulty, the virtue that is often nowadays called "resilience."

But today, it seems that along with a wide latitude for pupils in choosing a course of study, teaching and learning must be purged of difficulty, to increase access and equality and even to remove any possibility of upset, as if pupil welfare is served by the removal of all challenge. Here, again, talk of "value" can easily decline into the economic and financial value of the ends to which academic courses lead. But the value of the Catholic curriculum is not simply in any material "success" that emerges; the value will be in the way the exercise of virtue helps to form the persons (both teachers and pupils) engaged in the process of study. One such academic virtue was identified by Simone Weil as *attention*, which we have discussed as a characteristically Benedictine quality under the rubric of *attentiveness*: "If however we consider the occupations in themselves, studies are nearer to God because of the attention which is their soul."[12] Both love of God and love of neighbor can be found in the process of study, if conceived of as a journey towards the good — which is God. Writing a good essay, reading a good book, painting a good picture, listening to a good piece of music: in the Catholic curriculum the pupil experiences those terms that are part of the common parlance of school — "good" and "very good" — as loaded with ultimate, transcendent meaning. The love of learning is bound up with the desire for the good.

TRUTH

The Christian vision shows us that reality, or truth, is personal. The Christ who is "the way, the truth, and the life" is also the Word of God who existed from the beginning. If "only God is good," we know truth in the person of the Son. If the Father brings the good into being through story (*mythos*), through utterance, it is in the Son (*logos*) that other beings come into existence and the thinking (dialectic) of other persons is made possible. Descartes

---

12   Simone Weil, "Reflections on the Right Use of School Studies with a View to the Love of God" (1942). http://www.hagiasophiaclassical.com/wp/wp-content/uploads/2012/10/Right-Use-of-School-Studies-Simone-Weil.pdf.

rightly recognized thinking as of the essence of the human person, even if he neglected other equally important aspects. The Catholic curriculum will foster in the young this reflection on the nature of things, out of the desire to understand what is true. As Pope John Paul II famously put it: "Faith and reason are like two wings on which the human spirit rises to the contemplation of truth; and God has placed in the human heart a desire to know the truth — in a word, to know himself — so that, by knowing and loving God, men and women may also come to the fullness of truth about themselves."[13] Human growth and personal fulfillment are intrinsically bound up with our relationship with the truth, just as human degradation is bound up with the power of that which is false: false narratives, false language, and false images. An education in virtue will seek to enable pupils to be able to exercise a healthy skepticism towards the values of "the world," and this will involve the development of the reason, not understood as a mental faculty only but as involving the right habits of the heart that enable us to listen and discern deeply. The dialectic of different voices includes both the true and the false, and the Catholic curriculum needs to provide the means by which the young can tell truth from falsity.

Young people hear many different voices in their diverse, pluralistic, and multicultural world. They encounter different stories, competing narratives, and alternative views. The shared stories and common meaning upon which religion relies no longer occupy secure and privileged positions of authority. Language itself, in which the stories are told, resolves into various registers, jargons, and argots, with imposed (and self-imposed) limitations provided by various powerful ideologies of race, gender, and sex. The young are naturally concerned to pursue goodness and make ethical decisions, but when the culture they inhabit has become detached from religion, and the experience of religion by the young necessarily very limited, then the context in which "truth" is considered

---

13   John Paul II, *Fides et Ratio*. http://w2.vatican.va/content/john-paul-ii/en/encyclicals/documents/hf_jp-ii_enc_14091998_fides-et-ratio.html.

becomes ideological and politicized; in postmodernity, it becomes highly relative and subjective.

While concepts of what is truthful, therefore, can be studied philosophically in the classroom, more important is formation in the truth, and in this a more fruitful context is the literary and the historical. It is no accident, in a time when religion has declined into a minority activity, that fantasy is so appealing as a literary genre, and especially to the young. Like fairy stories, fantasy provides narratives of meaning and shared experience. The value of stories is not only in revealing the fundamental relevance of *mythos* and *logos* to human beings; within the Catholic curriculum, literature and history can begin the process in the hearts and minds of the young that returns them to the truest of true stories, one that is both fairy-tale and history. Fairy-tale, wrote Tolkien, "does not deny the existence of *dyscatastrophe*, of sorrow and failure: the possibility of these is necessary to the joy of deliverance; it denies (in the face of much evidence, if you will) universal final defeat and in so far is *evangelium*, giving a fleeting glimpse of Joy, Joy beyond the walls of the world, poignant as grief."[14] One way of making sense for the young of the greatest story ever told is through the medium of the stories that most attract them, for "the peculiar quality of the 'joy' in successful Fantasy can thus be explained as a sudden glimpse of the underlying reality or truth."[15] That Tolkien was a Catholic writer is also an interesting, though secondary, theme for a literature course in a Catholic school; the primary point here is that in revealing aspects of the truth of the human condition, the study of literature can be connected both to the actual reading experience of the young and to the larger religious context.

A parallel perspective on the subject of history can be found, for example, in the work of Christopher Dawson, who within a Catholic curriculum can provide an alternative to the prevailing grand narrative known as the "Whig interpretation of history," which sees

14   Tolkien, 75.
15   Ibid., 77.

a "progress" (a scientifically necessary one, in its Marxist versions) of knowledge and liberty emerging in the modern period out of the medieval wreckage of Catholic obscurantism. The history of the Church, in this prevailing view, is one of ignorance and repression; the Church is always behind the times, clinging in its patriarchal way to power and peddling fantastical lies in the face of scientific truth. A considerable, self-conscious effort within the Catholic curriculum must be made therefore towards a counter-cultural view of history, since all sorts of presuppositions will be found in the standard materials in textbooks and syllabi, alongside a methodology based on the scientific method, which in a scientistic age is seen as the only way of confirming the truth. And just as there were Catholic historians, such as Dawson, so were there Catholic scientists, such as the Augustinian friar Gregor Mendel ("the father of modern genetics"), or Georges Lemaitre, the Belgian priest, astronomer, and physicist. Among Benedictines, there have been Stanley Jaki, the Hungarian theologian and physicist,[16] and in the eighteenth century the Benedictines in Germany, such as the Scottish-born Ildephons Kennedy and Benedict Arbuthnot, who made considerable contributions to science and mathematics. Richard of Wallingford (1292–1336), Abbot of St Albans, was a noted mathematician and astronomer, best known for the astronomical clock he designed. Today, Fr Cyprian Weaver of St John's Abbey, Minnesota, is a Professor in the Department of Medicine at the University of Minnesota. The works of Newton and Einstein also show a religious vision of the workings of nature, as Dawson's was a religious vision of the workings of human history. To seek to show the young that the religious vision is not antithetical to a historically or scientifically true account of the world is to be counter-cultural, and such is the need to be met in the Catholic curriculum in the twenty-first century.

The idea of truth in a post-Christian and postmodern age is itself counter-cultural, especially if we do indeed live in a

16   See Stacy Trasancos, *Science Was Born of Christianity: The Teaching of Fr. Stanley L. Jaki* (The Habitation of Chimham Publishing, 2014).

"post-truth" culture. But how to enable the young to be skeptical of some of the stories, narratives, and accounts that the culture presents them with, without reinforcing the arid skepticism that underlies the culture? Is the Christian account of things not to be taken as merely one voice among many? Western secular liberalism implies that it is, and indeed it places itself above all religions in its advocacy of tolerance, reasonableness, and material comfort and prosperity — all maintained within a positivistic understanding of law as what the "majority" seems to want at any given time. All this implies that truth is malleable, varying according to individuals and circumstances, and therefore transitory and unstable. Such an idea of truth, essentially a "post-truth truth," will be rightly seen as debilitating and provoke a reactive desire in the young for some form of authority. In the universities, this has involved a recourse to the authority of identity ideology, and its associated rhetoric that promotes an anti-dialectic of the refusal to listen, to hear or to accept the claims of reason at all. Language itself has to be modified to accommodate identity ideology for fear of impinging on the autonomous worlds that individuals have become. The Christian worldview is becoming the most unacceptable narrative in this educational world where no one, not even the old-school rationalists and feminists, are safe. The formative influence, therefore, of the Catholic curriculum — as a place where the training in methods of argument and persuasion, of reasoning and presenting a case occur — needs to be re-lit by faith and imagination, partly in order to keep faith and imagination alive. Without these things, concepts of truth itself, and how it makes for the integrated human person that was once the promise of a liberal education, will likely disappear beneath political ideology.

Language can indeed be used reductively, as St Benedict implies in his Rule. It is as if Benedict's idea of *murmuring*, the promotion of private grievances and agendas of power, now constitutes the whole of modern higher-educational discourse. The focus is on what is lacking, imagined vacuities of loss, rather than on gratitude for the given. If the young are to be able to use language to build up rather than to break down (or *deconstruct*), then they need models from the religious and humane world, both past and present. Truth cannot be reduced to information, data, evidence, or even knowledge. Nothing can lead us to truth but wisdom, that which always has seemed folly to the world, which continues in ever-new forms of its old pride. The discourse of wisdom is always an argument with, as well as inside, the culture, a disputation with the entropic tendencies working against the integrity of truth. Wisdom tells us that truth is not abstract, because reality is personal; truth, therefore, is to be found not in *propositions* but in *dispositions* of persons towards other persons — even those with whom we happen to disagree. The contrary is the shrill cacophony of the Twittersphere, where truth is lost, and William Blake's insight is proved again and again:

> A truth that's told with bad intent
> Beats all the lies you can invent.[17]

BEAUTY

If it is the case that our condition in postmodernity is one where we are "after virtue" and "post-truth," so also has there been a "flight from beauty," as Roger Scruton has put it, in a culture of desecration. Young people are most likely to encounter a version of beauty in imagery of physical perfection, artificially enhanced and artificially constructed. Beauty exists in highly sexualized images which lack the radiance that reveals the sacred. Beauty may be associated with a physical perfectionism[18] that will always be beyond their reach, unattainable because unaffordable. Here again value becomes measured in material and financial terms. In a materialistic culture, it follows that beauty will be seen solely in physical and material terms, but beauty has a deeper reality than the physical. Beauty can "take in just

---

17   Blake, "Auguries of Innocence."
18   See Will Storr, *Selfie: How We Became Self-Obsessed and What It's Doing to Us* (London: Picador, 2017).

about every ontological category (there are beautiful propositions as well as beautiful worlds, beautiful proofs as well as beautiful snails, even beautiful diseases and beautiful deaths)."[19] The good, the true, and the beautiful exist in each other, and beauty is especially pervasive of goodness and truth; Aquinas spoke of it as a property of the transcendentals, rather than a transcendental itself. In that sense, beauty is like the Spirit, the breath of the Father that gives shape and form, harmony and order, and also radiance and glory. The human desire for beauty is ultimately not simply a delight in external forms. Beauty is sacramental in showing how order, proportion, justness, and sweetness, the right and the fitting, reveal ultimate value in God. A curriculum with no place for beauty would have something fundamental missing, and subjects which do not relate their matter to beauty (where appropriate) would also be lacking. The sense of beauty relates to both what is true and what is good in the person and in society.

It is in the sphere of the visual arts that the Catholic curriculum has a particular role, and can be especially redemptive. Young people today live in a world of images, even more than words. They can be enslaved through images, or else images can be a source of freedom, a way to a new kind of seeing. Images proliferate in the digital world that the young inhabit. They make images of themselves to form part of their own story, shared with many others often hardly known to them, on social media. This story can be an expression of, or an alternative to, their own personhood. Young people will come across highly sexualized and pornographic images of desecration, beauty made ugly, in a repudiation of goodness and truth. Far from being peripheral, subjects such as art, design, and photography can help to educate the young in ways of seeing that reveal the human and the humane, rather than deface and reduce it. The human face is where the soul is most evident, and the word *person — persona*

19 Roger Scruton, *Beauty: A Very Short Introduction* (Oxford: Oxford University Press, 2011), 1.

originally meaning the mask that represented the character in Roman theater — represents the human identity and being of the self and of the other. No wonder, then, that the word *deface*, to besmirch or remove the face, is cognate with the fouling of the beautiful. The digital world of images is a very powerful one, and frequently devoid of the good and the true. It is a world that exerts its power most forcefully over the young, and unless it is engaged with at the deepest level (the theological and the philosophical) it will have increasingly destructive effects on the way that humanity and the human person are understood. Beauty also connects the human person with that which is outside the human: the beauty of the world around us, of nature as well as the built environment, revealing the sacred in all things. As Roger Scruton has put it: "environmental degradation comes in just the same way that moral degradation comes, through de-facing things — representing people and places in impersonal ways, as objects to be used rather than as subjects to be respected."[20] In the Catholic curriculum, all ways of seeing the world, through art, geography, and architecture, through the camera lens or the lens of the microscope, have the potential to reveal beauty.

Beauty can also be revealed through the ordering of words, which can also convey images and harmony and proportion through patterning in sound and meter. Pupils who are adept at recognizing and making patterns will have an affinity for both music and mathematics, such that the patterns in things can reveal to them the essential order of the cosmos. Scientific theories can possess elegance and harmony, expressed in words, figures, or symbols, and as such are another way of revealing the beauty of creation and the Creator. The poetic imagination can be an insight into the creative process, the mind of the Creator himself, as utterance accommodates itself to order and harmony. In this sense, the "sweetness and light" of the "best that has been thought and said"[21] are very valuable models for students wondering about

---

20   Roger Scruton, *The Face of God* (London: Continuum, 2012), 151.
21   See Matthew Arnold, *Culture and Anarchy* (1869).

the nature of God. The great books of literature, history, science, mathematics, or other subjects, and the great works in the history of art or music, are very much akin to religion and faith in revealing the face of God; Matthew Arnold was only wrong in thinking that high culture could substitute for religion rather than complement it. In a Catholic school, all the opportunities that present themselves to introduce young people to the glories of sacred art, in music, painting, or sculpture as well as in sacred poetry, enable the curriculum to set the wide parameters within which the beautiful is encountered. As Pope Benedict has written, "Whether it is Bach or Mozart that we hear in church, we have a sense in either case of what *gloria Dei*, the glory of God, means. The mystery of infinite beauty is there and enables us to experience the presence of God more truly and vividly than in many sermons."[22]

Beauty finds its deepest and most fitting expression in liturgy. Image, movement, and gesture here combine to provide an encounter, in space and time, with the divine. Liturgy is a transfiguration of human congregation through the agency of beauty, rather as sacred images involve a transfiguration. Pope Benedict again:

> For Plato, the category of the beautiful had been definitive. The beautiful and the good, ultimately the beautiful and God, coincide. Through the appearance of the beautiful we are wounded in our innermost being, and that wound grips us and takes us beyond ourselves; it stirs longing into flight and moves us toward the truly Beautiful, to the Good in itself. Something of this Platonic foundation lives on in the theology of icons, even though the Platonic ideas of the beautiful and of vision have been transformed by the light of Tabor.[23]

22 Cardinal Joseph Ratzinger, *The Spirit of the Liturgy*, trans. John Saward (San Francisco: Ignatius, 2000), 146.
23 Ibid., 126.

In congregational singing there is a powerful combination of words and music in a dramatic, personal participation in the order of creation, a physical and spiritual harmonizing of self with others, as also in the sitting, standing, bowing, kneeling, and crossing of liturgical enactment. This is the drama of monastic chant in the Liturgy of the Hours, a particular grace to which pupils and teachers in Benedictine monastic schools have access. Liturgical and ritual patterns emerge naturally from the natural experience of human beings. Young people take to them more easily than might be imagined, and they are an essential part of a Catholic school experience. At a subconscious or even conscious level, they are a way in which human beings become beautiful by participating in beauty.

The beauty to which each human being is called is most fully realized in the Blessed Virgin Mary. The most beautiful created being, as revealed in the greatest sacred art, is Our Lady, Virgin and Mother. The achievement of transcendent beauty (which is also goodness and truth) in the human by the Creator is in Mary, Mother of God. This astonishing unity of the human and the divine is also the image of the Catholic curriculum, of a Catholic education, that is, the Madonna and Child. As Seat of Wisdom, Mary is the patroness of the Catholic curriculum, and the transcendent beauty of the Mother of God, seen in countless examples from medieval and renaissance art, is expressed in the human face that looks towards us in love. Mary is the image of what the human can become through welcoming Christ into the heart of our being, and this image is also the promise and fulfillment of Catholic education.

CHAPTER 7
Co-curriculum

WORK AND PLAY

The co-curriculum is that part of a school's activity that typically takes place outside of the classroom and can include a range of educational experiences that are to some extent optional, which may harness particular enthusiasms of teachers and pupils and so give room for the expression and development of freedom. "Co-curricular" seems a more satisfactory adjective than the common alternative "extra-curricular," since the co-curriculum is as valuable, in educational terms, as the essentially academic curriculum. The co-curriculum can of course also include aspects of academic enrichment, but it also embraces drama, music, arts and crafts, and especially sport. There is an emphasis on *making* (and what we often call, perhaps too freely, *creativity*), as in play-making, music-making, producing a work of art or design, or seeking victory in individual or team contest. The co-curriculum is a temporal and physical place apart where leisure can be exercised to bring something good, true, and beautiful into being (even if for a limited time only, as in a concert) that was not there before. The co-curriculum includes therefore that most special form of individual and corporate leisure activity, the liturgy. The liturgical life of a Catholic school is an essential part of its co-curriculum and reflects the Divine Office that is at the heart of a monastery, itself described by St Benedict as a *schola dominici servitii*, a school of the Lord's service, or, as we have said, a leisure-place (*schola*) in which to serve the Lord. The co-curriculum dissolves the potential duality (and ultimately false dichotomy) of *work* and *play*. The work of God (*opus Dei*) is the highest form of leisure activity.

St. Benedict can seem to us to have firmly excluded any sense
of play from his Rule, although he has provided a time and a place
for art, writing, and crafts, in addition to the singing in choir: here
is where the essence of what we mean by play can be found in
a monastery, as it must be found in any broadly humane way of
living because it is essential to human existence. In his ground-
breaking study *Homo Ludens: A Study of the Play-Element in Culture*
(1949), Johan Huizinga wrote:

> Summing up the formal characteristics of play we might
> call it a free activity standing quite consciously outside
> "ordinary life" as being "not serious," but at the same time
> absorbing the player intensely and utterly. It is an activ-
> ity connected with no material interest, and no profit
> can be gained by it. It proceeds within its own proper
> boundaries of time and space according to fixed rules
> and in an orderly manner. It promotes the formation of
> social groups which tend to surround themselves with
> secrecy and to stress their difference from the common
> world by disguise or other means.[1]

The characteristics of play, as Huizinga identifies them above,
have obvious connections with the sacred and the transcendent,
and the element of fantasy (or imagination) present in the act of
play is the means by which the player takes himself into another
sphere of being. The similarities between play and religion, specifically liturgy, may easily be discerned; Huizinga was very aware
of them himself, and early in his book cites Romano Guardini's famous work *The Spirit of the Liturgy* (1918). There, Guardini
devotes a chapter to "The Playfulness of the Liturgy," and he
emphasizes the gratuitous. Like a work of art, "the liturgy has no
purpose, or, at least, it cannot be considered from the standpoint
of purpose. It is not a means which is adapted to attain a certain

---

1   Johan Huizinga, *Homo Ludens: A Study of the Play-Element in Culture* (Kettering, OH: Angelico Press, 2016), 13.

end."[2] In the co-curriculum, as in the liturgy, the pupil is in the realm of the free and imaginative capacities that can help him to appreciate the value of that which is beyond the utilitarian and workaday world.

In cultures where children (and many adults) do little or no physical work, physical play in sport and exercise of various kinds becomes a crucial way of promoting the health of the young. The old adage *mens sana in corpore sano* may hold wisdom for an age in which not only the physical but also the mental health of the young becomes of more and more concern. Physical play involves its own ordering of itself that, we might reasonably assume, helps develop the good order not only of the body and mind but also of the soul. In this sense, the sacredness of games and sporting exercise lies deep within human experience, very evident in the ancient worlds of Greece and Rome. The ideas of both *paideia* and *agon* are rooted deeply in the sacred. Play and contest have essential significance still in a Christian education, which must also be fully humane, and their importance and depth of meaning are referenced when St Paul writes to Timothy: "I have fought the good fight to the end; I have run the race to the finish; I have kept the faith; all there is to come for me now is the crown of uprightness which the Lord, the upright judge, will give to me on that Day."[3] The image is more than a convenient metaphor. Games enact the contest and struggle that exist in every person's life, and just as theater enacts human life experience in a way that makes for the emotional health of the audience (and also the actors), so physical exertion, teamwork, the common pursuit, self-discipline and ordering, trust and mutual reliance and support are all spiritual and moral benefits that arise from involvement in sporting activity. Modern childhood and adolescence — sedentary, over-protected from struggle, atomized — need

---

2 Romano Guardini, *The Spirit of the Liturgy*, trans. Ada Lane (New York, NY: Crossroad Publishing Co., 1997), 66. It should be noted that Guardini's highly influential study was in some ways a Benedictine project, written at the invitation of Abbot Ildephons Herwegen of Maria Laach Abbey.

3 2 Timothy 4:7–8.

an education of the body as well as the soul, mind, and heart.

The co-curriculum is thus a place where the attributes of play, in Huizinga's definition, are experienced and exercised. Freedom, order, space, and time are experienced in a purposeful way of doing good with, and for, others. The co-curriculum can become a transitional, liminal space between classroom and world outside, in which the exercise of imaginative sympathies opens up possibilities. Chosen or acquired enthusiasms become a way in which to think about the future. Robert Frost speaks, in "Two Tramps in Mud Time," of a resolution of the work-play distinction:

> But yield who will to their separation,
> My object in living is to unite
> My avocation and my vocation
> As my two eyes make one in sight.
> Only where love and need are one,
> And the work is play for mortal stakes,
> Is the deed ever really done
> For heaven and the future's sakes.[4]

The forward dynamic of human living seems to rely, Frost suggests, on the difference between work and play disappearing when one is working (or playing) at the deepest level, and when an activity is most engaging, imaginative, and in harmony with the creative principle at the heart of things. (Again, in Benedictine life this is most readily seen in the *Opus Dei* of the Divine Office.) In addition, "avocation" might be a way for the young to find their "vocation." Vocation must engage the heart if it is to move into the future, and bring that future itself into being. Our "love" is our "need" and vice versa.

The kind of play that liturgy will most immediately remind us of is drama. Play-making in schools is at least as old as Shakespeare, who would have acted in plays at the grammar school

---

4   Robert Frost, *The Poetry of Robert Frost* (New York, NY: Holt, Rinehart and Winston, 1969), 277.

in Stratford-upon-Avon. When the young participate in school drama they exercise so many useful faculties that it is difficult to think of a more broadly educational single experience. Pupils memorize, visualize, vocalize; they "play their part" in order to support others; they must be punctual and committed and work hard physically, mentally, and emotionally; they learn to be a reliable individual in a team effort. They also learn, through adopting *personae*, about identity, imaginatively becoming a different human being. Watching or participating in dramas on religious subjects, they enter into the spiritual experience of other lives, and this can awaken their own. In its origins in ancient Greece, the drama is of course intimately connected with sacred ritual, and in its similarity to liturgy can help the young, as they participate in both, to understand the purpose of liturgy as a re-enactment of human (and, in Christ, divine) experience. As Guardini put it, "The liturgy has laid down the serious rules of the sacred game which the soul plays before God."[5]

MUSIC, ART, AND CRAFT

Music, art, and design may all of course be studied as part of the academic curriculum, but they also exist, in their "avocational" sense, in the co-curriculum. In their relation to beauty, they are closely bound up with the workings of the human heart, and its desire. Music occupies such an essential part in Benedictine life and education that it is impossible to imagine an authentically Benedictine school without it. In the chant of the office, and later developments in the work of St. Gregory the Great, Benedictine music evokes the Christian vision of creation as a beautiful *cosmos*, as opposed to the modern suspicion of nature as a rude *chaos*. As Katherine Le Mée has put it, "the act of singing has the effect of opening up peace in the mind and heart,"[6] a space which

---

5   Guardini, 7.

6   Katherine Le Mée, *The Benedictine Gift to Music* (New York, NY: Paulist Press, 2003), 212.

the peace of God enters. But chant has the effect of reordering or recalibrating not only the mind and the heart, but also the body. Just as ancient reading was an activity for the body, such that words become things made of breath by the workings of the chest, so is the activity of the choir. The experience of music is an educating of the human being in a way that, albeit not occupying the discursive intellect, takes the soul into the ordering creative life of the *Logos*.[7] The "music of the spheres" is the phrase from medieval culture that sums up this beautiful order with love as its source. An education of the young that does not include music, then, is radically incomplete.

Katherine Le Mée argues that the ancient wisdom which says that music can reflect the order at the heart of things finds expression in the octave, a model that comes down to us from the ancient Egyptians. The eight-point pattern may also have come from music into the structures of the Divine Office, the liturgical year, and the Mass itself. Indeed, "Boris Mouravieff, who placed himself in the Russian Orthodox tradition, believed that the octave could be taken as a useful framework or model to make sense of the unfolding of significant activities that form a whole."[8] *Do* is an end and a beginning, containing the whole; *Re* is a step forward, a first move; *Mi* is the result of confident resolve; *Fa* takes more effort, often a pause, perhaps needing courage; *Sol* comes from a newer confidence born of knowing we can make it; *La* is more subdued, perhaps sad, where we can again feel unsure of our way and need more grace; *Si* (or *Ti*) is a kind of falling forward towards the line, in joy as the goal (*Do* again) is reached. "The ascent of the octave," says Le Mée, represents a "drawing near to God,"[9] and the eight-part structure is full of Biblical number symbolism, as is the four-part structure of *lectio divina*, as we have seen. Eight is seven (the number of perfection) plus one (a new beginning). The connections between music and mathematics are manifold, but

---

7 It is no accident that some creation myths, including Tolkien's in *The Silmarillion*, see cosmos emerging from divine music.

8 Le Mée, 63.

9 Ibid., 213.

the sacred link connecting them, and connecting them in human experience, is one that the young would benefit from hearing in the context of a Catholic and Benedictine education; it might never appear to them elsewhere.

What is true of the monastic approach to music is also true of monastic art in general. As Le Mée says:

> The particular kind of beauty seen in monastic art is active and dynamic and yet always contains an element of interior silence and peace of heart. The work itself is seen as a continuation of the creative activity of God, bestowing on whatever the form may be — music, architecture, painting, sculpture, handwork — a supplemental beauty. The quality of the particular endeavor is often the result of the labor of a small group working anonymously with charity, humility, organization, and obedience presupposed.[10]

If we think, for instance, of the art of the school of the Abbey of Beuron, in southern Germany, or a medieval book of hours or Gospels; or even, into modern times, the craft of a Benedictine liturgy or homily, we will note qualities of precision, luminosity, durability, integrity, and humanity. The art and craft reflect the virtues of a certain kind of life that is intended to reveal the divine in the human. Le Mée quotes the composer John Tavener: "We are creatures that point to our Creator. The modernist has already set *himself* up as 'creator,' he has wiped God out of the picture. It is just a dialogue between him and the synthesizer."[11] In contrast, art in the Benedictine tradition reflects the reality of a world where the essential form and content all come from God.

In the Benedictine arts and crafts tradition we see the epitome of a Catholic regard for skill and utility. The emphasis on the value of the liberal arts, especially after Newman, could lead us to identify a Catholic education with the academic and the

10 Ibid., 127.
11 Ibid., 210.

classical in a way rather too exclusive. In "Technical Education and Its Relation to Science and Literature" (1932), the English philosopher Alfred North Whitehead wrote that "the antithesis between a technical and a liberal education is fallacious. There can be no adequate technical education which is not liberal, and no liberal education which is not technical: that is, no education which does not impart both technique and intellectual vision."[12] Whitehead credited the Benedictines with bringing about a synthesis of the liberal and the servile arts, and held up the Benedictine example in a critique of modern approaches to technical education: "If, in the troubled times which may be before us, you wish appreciably to increase the chance of some savage upheaval, introduce widespread technical education and ignore the Benedictine ideal. Society will then get what it deserves."[13] Western society has ignored the Benedictine ideal of work being intrinsically bound up with our deepest joy, and it has rather fostered the identification of labor and grief, which can only be avoided in what actually represents an empty and shallow understanding of leisure. Without the religious vision, it is difficult to make things well, in any sense.

To reveal the Good, the True, and the Beautiful, skill and utility must, the Benedictine tradition suggests, be enlightened by the religious vision, that is, the religious imagination. There is a restraint and discipline, a simplicity and formality about Christian art in the Benedictine tradition,[14] which shows us the value of art being taught in school. The forms and conventions help us to see truly, by bringing shape and form to the human imagination. Again, we come across something counter-cultural. Art in schools today will likely follow secular, modernist conventions in

12 A. N. Whitehead, *The Aims of Education and Other Essays* (London: Williams and Northgate Ltd., 1932), 74.

13 Ibid., 68–9.

14 The art and craft of Beuron seem emblematic here. There are such things as Benedictine churches built in the Baroque style, but they seem exceptional somehow, rather than typically Benedictine, however inclusive that category might be.

which pupils are encouraged to be "creative" and "express themselves," at which point they imagine modernist works reflecting
the free-floating self: convention cannot be easily escaped. Man
cannot create *ex nihilo*, and can only imitate; and so the question
appears of what to copy. In a Catholic and Benedictine context,
one would hope for models from nature or from sacred art—the
nearest human beings can come to the Creator and his genuine creativity. The Christian imagination will be fostered and
educated by the best models if it is to become truly free, and
capable of being new. Authentic Christian art is always reflective
of the freedom of the artist, the kind of freedom that the Victorian critic of art and society John Ruskin saw in the craftsmen
who worked on the great Gothic cathedrals of Catholic Europe.
The Gothic (unlike Classical architecture) Ruskin saw as truly
Christian because it was made by free men, and its style fostered
their freedom. A whole way of living, a whole society in all its
political, theological, and philosophical ramifications could be
seen, Ruskin thought, in the stones of medieval Gothic cathedrals.

SERVICE AND SOCIETY

Part of the "play" of the co-curriculum can be in providing opportunities to pupils for engaging in real work and service in the local
community. The co-curricular program of a Catholic and Benedictine school will include work with the poor, the marginalized,
and the homeless, some of whom may be economic migrants,
refugees, or asylum seekers. Pupils will also find opportunities to
support charities, and charity shops, to learn of work with prisoners and those suffering from addiction. They can learn to work
with younger children in primary schools, or the elderly in care
homes. These experiences can become linked to learning about
enterprise and entrepreneurship, as exercises in the interface
between charity and business. The curriculum that includes religion, ethics, economics, and politics can find practical expression
in the co-curriculum, and the profound critique of modernity that
exists in Catholic Social Teaching (anticipated by figures such as

Ruskin, and complemented by others such as Schumacher) can be discovered in action. The co-curriculum is the interface between the school and the world, and can be a place where vocation is discovered and an interaction between the young and the adult world finds a wider expression. Pupils also have a reason to work with each other to bring projects to completion, and these projects may also be intimately bound up with the New Evangelization. Faith begets works, and perhaps, vice versa, faith may be discovered in the encounters that come with active service.

In the co-curriculum, especially, pupils learn that leadership is primarily concerned with taking responsibility for others, rather than enjoying status or exercising power. A striking example of pupil leadership is to be found at St Benedict's, Newark, New Jersey, a school that, as we have seen, epitomizes Pope Francis's vision of the Church as a "field hospital."[15] Senior pupils there exercise real responsibility for younger pupils, including in a pastoral sense of showing practical solicitude for their welfare. The mission of healing is not restricted, however, to empathy or sympathy: the experience of school is geared towards building resilience of heart, body, mind, and soul. For pupils in more privileged schools, the experience of reaching out into the wider community is one of broadening the understanding and experience of a human society fraught with social ills, including downward spirals of dependency. The Benedictine monastery-school is accustomed to seeing itself as a hospital, a place both of welcome and of healing, one which is also (however temporarily for some) an experience of home. In modernity, homelessness is an existential state that can include people (both children and adults) of all classes, conditions, and nationalities. Reaching out into the community is an act of welcoming into the home, the base-hospital of the school community in which not only are the members of the school served, and serve each other, but they serve the wider world, not only in the future but also in the present.

15 Cf. Convery, Franchi and McCluskey, *Reclaiming the Piazza II: Catholic Education and the New Evangelisation* (Leominster: Gracewing, 2017), 28.

Pupils' experience of community service is perhaps most successful when it is seen as an exchange of gifts. An example of this working in practice can be seen in the co-curricular program of the school of São Bento in Brazil, discussed above. The danger of charitable work is the objectification of the recipient, who is confirmed in victimhood. A more enlightened and humane model is that of an encounter between subjects and the sharing of experience, a mutual accompaniment. In a world of displacement (which includes those displaced within their own country, as well as those displaced from their country — not to mention displacement as an existential problem for many people in modernity), charitable exchange becomes a way of alleviating the loss of home by establishing a focus of neighborhood in which new homes (temporary or permanent) can be established. Both the very young and the very old can experience the worst effects of displacement and deprivation, especially in a modern city such as Rio de Janeiro, which acutely displays the symptoms of modern displacement seen in so many Western towns and cities. Care for the vulnerable begins in the restoration of humanity, which is also the development of humane instincts in young adults.

The gratuitousness of service[16] is perhaps its most important lesson for those people who carry it out in the context of the school co-curriculum. Far from being a dispensable add-on, the experience of the gratuitous takes the young into the very heart of their own being, created not to serve the uses of impersonal power, but to serve God in complete freedom. Existence is the gratuitous gift of the Creator to his creature. Here, again, service can be likened to play, which also entails the gratuitous. So many of the activities in school that we associate with "play" — musical, sporting, dramatic — can be brought into the context of community service: musical and theatrical performances for the elderly, sports coaching for the very young, and so forth, all bring into

16   Cf. Benedict XVI, *Deus Caritas Est.* http://w2.vatican.va/content /benedict-xvi/en/encyclicals/documents/hf_ben-xvi_enc_20051225_deus -caritas-est.html.

the encounter between persons a spirit of life and joy, a sharing in the fruits of creative living. Young and old complement each other by bringing what the other lacks; hope and promise are exchanged for resilience and experience. Participation in service activities in the local community becomes an extension of pupils' human experience outside of the tightly controlled world of home and school and digital social network. Pupils meet people they might otherwise be unlikely to meet — people of different ages and experiences, whose very existence and need challenge limited notions of what it is to be human. The lesson for the young is that home cannot be taken for granted, either as comfortable or as problematic, but it is built out of human interactions generously and gratuitously made in a spirit of love.

A pupil's service in society, then, can be summarized as learning how to make a home. It is learning that to be human is to live as a subject in a world of subjects. This is the "I-thou" relationship that is distinct from our relations in the world of objects, characterized by "I-it": much of what is wrong in human life lies in the confusion of the two. Since Christ is in the "I-thou" sphere of our relationships, as the knowledge of Christ recedes so do our "I-thou" relationships resemble more and more "I-it." But since one cannot have a satisfactory relationship with an object, the "I" recedes into itself and people come to resemble disconnected subjects unable to enter into relationship. This is problematic for human beings, who are naturally relational, and in modernity the problem is answered by ideology: how do we maintain a functioning society of isolated individuals? Modernity has thrown up all sorts of political answers to this problem of man-in-the-mass, the most recent being to see individuals situated in interest groups based on sex, creed, and color and their various subdivisions, locked in a zero-sum game of competing interests. With the subsidiary forms from which traditional society has been composed (marriage, family, neighborhood, parish, voluntary associations, local government) made out of "I-thou" relationships, now on the wane, a coercive state seeks to appease interest groups made up of unrelated individuals. It is as if the displaced gods of the household wander like refugees from somewhere to nowhere. In such a world, what should the young learn about the nature of human society so that it might be remade?

COMMUNITY AND COMMUNION

We hear the word *community* spoken a good deal today, but frequently it is used to mean "interest group," a group of individuals with claims against the interests of other groups, expressed in the language of "rights." Rights are "fought" for, either in a metaphorical or literal sense, in an ongoing antagonism of black against white, woman against man, gay against heterosexual, Muslim against Christian, and so on. Ethnic minorities form "communities" within nations, various voluntary associations become "communities"; people in the same profession or trade become a "community." These are very loose senses of the word that elide the fact that real communities are formed not out of single shared interests but out of a totality of shared language, customs, beliefs, stories, kinship, and experience, usually in a particular place and over many generations. In short, communities need a household which is the incarnation of the idea of home. So much of modern culture works against enduring community because it takes little account of, or actively works against, the human need for shared forms of goodness, truth, and beauty in families and neighborhoods. Where once the effect of Christianity on the tribes of Europe was a weakening of the exclusive community ties of kinship — as in the effect of monastic communities on their various localities, such that the stranger could be admitted and find a home — nowadays a new kind of tribalism, based on the exclusive common interest, threatens to undermine the real ways in which human communities form and grow.

Community finds its life not in ideology but in human relationships. The co-curriculum of the school is where the real nature of community is encountered, learned, and enacted. Much of the co-curriculum is organized in a way that reflects the voluntary associations of civil society: clubs, societies, teams, prayer groups, study groups. Traditional civil society enables the acceptance and integration of the stranger, whereas the ideology of victimhood erects and maintains barriers. The effect, then, of the co-curriculum in a Catholic and Benedictine school is counter-cultural and non-ideological. By engaging in works of service in the local community, young people gain a direct experience of how communities are built, rather than simply valuing community as a concept. In the encounter with persons (which constitutes the beginnings of communion) kinship or tribalism (of class, race, gender, or aspects of religious identification) is replaced with fellowship, friendship, and neighborliness. In a pluralist society, the future can be a retreat into tribalism or a walking forward with others into communion when the ties that bind become a means to affirming a common humanity rather than a means of exclusion. Government-sponsored citizenship programs also seek to promote in the young a civic-minded spirit of engagement and cooperation. The secular state and the religious school pursue parallel paths and have similar aims. But the religious motivation to voluntary association and charitable service can mitigate the impact of (while never being entirely immune from) the structures of power that hide behind charitable work and can enable exploitation and abuse. Without the reality of communion at the heart of service in the community, and the free, gratuitous, and mutual engagement of persons that is necessary for communion, charity can become the exercise of power in another form of patronage, which is the opposite of fellowship.

The Catholic and Benedictine school, as a form of household like the monastery, provides in itself many opportunities for the learning of fellowship. As in ancient times, when the principles, conventions, and customs of the household had to be preserved by the monasteries, so nowadays schools are expected to make up the social deficit in the things that make for good community living. As we have noted, the Roman *familia* was more than the blood-ties of some of its members, but meant rather the whole base-community of the household, including all those who lived and worked and depended on the success of the whole. Schools today model the attributes of the good household in which the work of all (cooks, cleaners, maintenance staff, those who care for the grounds, who drive the buses, who maintain the computer and phone networks) is recognized and valued. All adults working in a school bear some responsibility to teach, in the widest sense of the word. The experience by the young of the work of support staff is part of their education, teaching them how the individual relies on the work of the whole community. Often the co-curriculum provides opportunities for the support staff and the pupils to meet on a different basis, such as with cooks in cooking clubs or grounds staff in gardening clubs. The "hidden curriculum" of pupils' experience in school is enriched by the wide variety of persons and work that is needed to make the whole household, the model community of school, work. The school community can also be a place where displaced persons find a new role in a new household.

A sign of community is the place at table. The English word *company* has within it the Latin particle *cum* (with) and the noun *panis* (bread). It is in the nature of the common life of human beings to sit and share bread together. Sadly, the way food is eaten nowadays, both in school and elsewhere, is utilitarian rather than sacramental. Educational institutions often run on cafeterias rather than on shared dishes and table service as in a monastic community. But, nonetheless, "table-fellowship" (sometimes missing in houses and families) is of natural importance to the young, and to watch a school refectory at mealtime is to see the extraordinary ability of human beings to achieve order. The young in a cafeteria can learn to include those who might otherwise have to find a table on their own, although they can also divide themselves into cliques and friendship groups that consciously exclude. The coming together at table is not necessarily graced by prayer, and good manners and healthy eating are not so easily supervised. Staff usually sit separately from pupils. So even when cafeteria-style eating is unavoidable for reasons of space and time, Catholic and Benedictine schools will find opportunities for more formal dining in houses or year groups, on feast days or at regular intervals. Whenever schools gather for assemblies, for worship, for meals, the sacramental aspect of any community activity should be revealed.

The co-curriculum, then, is the essential space in which the young learn of the interrelationship between work and play, duty and free choice, study and leisure, solemnity and joy. A sense of ritual and of the liturgical permeates all that is done in the practice of human living. In the experience of communion between persons, the nature of human community is understood and lived out as an encounter. The full implications and ramifications of the word *communication* are also learned as involving language but not being confined to language. As young people spend more and more time in the world of digital communication, attention needs to be given to the ways in which digital technology promotes the human or the anti-human. The choice is between service on the one hand and power on the other. Human society might be complemented, extended, or enriched by the capacities of digital technology, but it can also be experienced thereby as narrow, transient, and unforgiving. Online "communities" may be where the young tend to live, mentally and emotionally, but the digital world may be at a further remove from the already de-sacralized culture of modernity. The household of the school, and its reaching out into the life of the local community, can be a counter-cultural experience of personal encounter, an encounter with the really human.

CHAPTER 8
Living

RELATIONSHIP

In any place of learning there exists a "hidden curriculum" made up of the daily interactions among pupils, within their families, and with teachers and other adults they meet on the way through their daily routine. Much of pupils' communication with peers is via social media, and this part of their autonomous lives may be completely hidden from the adults responsible for them. The adults are immersed in the digital world, too, and may spend little time speaking with young people directly, except in the formal situations of lessons. The hidden curriculum includes also the ways in which individual pupils think and feel about their interactions with others, successfully mediated (or not) by a developing spiritual, intellectual, and moral life. Frequently, the young (like adults) come to their daily life in a state of woundedness, the result of family tensions or breakdown; precipitate decisions might have been made on social media which bring unforeseen and apparently catastrophic consequences; the magnified, scrutinized, and seemingly irrevocable consequences of each step they take in a surveillance world bring constant anxiety; the mysterious workings of their own affections disturb them; and questions of identity — questions about who *I* am, and who *you* are, are ever present. The young are aware of having to exert a great deal of control in the places (real and virtual) where they live, and the permanence of their digital record seems at odds with the transactional and transient world of the real people around them. It is in this frequently inhumane environment that the Catholic and Benedictine school seeks to point out the way to be fully human.

Adolescence is marked by a special intensity of emotional experience, such that relationships with others become at times the most important things in the young person's life; all else — academic achievement, career prospects, the approval of those adults in positions of responsibility for them — takes a secondary position, and indeed crucially depends for its effect on the personal and relational conduits of the young persons themselves. In this setting, as in the context of the digital world that problematizes relationships, those responsible for the pastoral care and guidance of the young should place the fostering of relationships in a curricular program of education in *friendship*. "As Aristotle puts it, 'Friendship is necessary to life, since no one would choose to live without friends even if he had all other material goods. Friends are a refuge in times of poverty and misfortune, they help guard the young from error, they help the old in their weakness, and help those in the prime of life to perform noble actions.'"[1] In the Christian vision, this basic human reality is further deepened: "Friendship in its highest or truest sense is shared personal life constituted by an equal and mutual relationship of unselfish love."[2] This idea of friendship, then, not only challenges superficial notions of who my friends are in a world of Facebook "friends"; it is a way of interpreting and transfiguring all our relationships — natural, professional, chosen, or given.

One of the most important aims, then, of the pastoral care in any school is helping the young to develop an understanding of themselves in relationship with others. In some educational contexts, pastoral care works as a way of facilitating the pupil's wishes, building self-esteem so that he can be whoever he wants to be, in a society of entitlements. This is seen as a supportive approach, encouraging ambitions and dreams of self-realization, but it can (whether the person is successful or not) simply reinforce isolation, or even egotistical narcissism. The "integral formation of persons" at the heart of pastoral practice in a Catholic

---

1   Aristotle, *Nicomachean Ethics* VIII.1, quoted in Jones and Barrie, 24.
2   Jones and Barrie, 25.

school helps young people to instead become habituated in the virtues, especially the theological virtues of *faith, hope,* and *charity,* and the cardinal virtues of *temperance, prudence, fortitude,* and *justice.* Such character-strengths enable the value-system or ethos of the school to reflect and sustain the education of the heart and help the young to see themselves as called to act virtuously in relation to others. In this way, they do not see themselves as passive recipients of values-based benefits existing either in the school or the wider society. Instead, they see the common good arising out of the active virtue of individual persons making good choices with regard to others. The central Benedictine virtue of humility inclines virtuous living towards service of others, and towards a realism about oneself that is the source of *resilience,* the new word for fortitude reflecting an emerging recognition that the welfare of the young depends not only on being surrounded by helping hands but (more importantly) on developing strength of character. The language of the virtues (and their opposite vices) is the trellis (*regula*) that supports the growth of the young person, a framework for good discipline and moderation in all things.

Reflection on the virtues as a framework for right relationships can also provide a context for "relationship and sex education" (RSE). In the secular world, sex education is primarily seen as an urgent necessity to be imposed on schools in order to counter sexually transmitted diseases, sexual abuse (especially of women and children), exploitation, and the sexualization of the digital world in which the young spend so much of their lives. What is not widely accepted in the world of secular education, however, is that the sexual threat to the young has its origins in the sexual revolution of the 1960's and the ideas of sexual freedom that emerged from it.[3] The young are encouraged to choose to pursue ethically "neutral" behavior and to be aware of the physical (and possibly mental) dangers of their choices. Their sexual behavior lies, along with all their other choices, in their sense of what is

---

3   See Gabriele Kuby, *The Global Sexual Revolution: Destruction of Freedom in the Name of Freedom* (Kettering, OH: Angelico Press, 2015).

right and good for them and makes for the satisfaction of their own needs and desires. On the contrary, Catholic sex education always sees the knowledge relating to sexual health as existing in the context of relationships, which come first. The knowledge of the workings of the human body needs to be transfigured by the theology of the body, if the body is not to be seen as an instrument of desire, or a machine for living in.[4] The prevalence of digital pornography is made possible by the wider cultural problem of the instrumentalization not only of bodies but of persons, and only an understanding of relationship will help young people to negotiate the threats that exist around them.

Pastoral care, then, is not so much about making pupils happy about the choices they make as about helping them to make happy choices. It is not about hedging them round so that they will never catch cold or need to decide when to take an overcoat with them. But while they will inevitably, and naturally, make their own decisions, they cannot be expected to do so, let alone in an informed manner, until they are equipped for the task. The integral formation of persons through habituation in the virtues gives an intellectual basis to ethical development and can be applied to practical examples that young people will face in their daily lives. Such development needs the leadership of teachers, tutors, guidance counselors, and older pupils in positions of responsibility — as well as parents. Although none of us can reasonably claim to be "formed," since formation as persons is never completed, the aim must be that the young become capable of commitment to others (including *another*) through learning about what makes for stability and fidelity in relationships. How to be a *friend* leads on to how to be a husband or a wife, which leads on to an understanding of how to be a father or a mother. And this is true also of priesthood and the religious life. In a contractual age, the qualitative difference of the vow (as opposed

---

4   This cultural disposition is explored in Richard Morgan's novel *Altered Carbon* (2002), now a Netflix series. In a dystopian future, human consciousness is stored in "cortical stacks" that can be put into a new body on the death of an old one, a process called "re-sleeving."

to the contract) as a supreme act of human freedom needs to be rediscovered. Just as the young need the stability and community of families and schools as means of their own flourishing, so the flourishing of society needs young people capable of building families and the other basic units of a community.

VOCATION AND IDENTITY

Our culture implies that our identity is self-selected and autonomously defined, the product of a certain understanding of freedom and choice. Ironically, such a self-definition is frequently bound up with ideologies of race, sexuality, and gender. In its most extreme form, such an understanding of identity can include fluidity, such as that one can decide on a different identity on a daily basis. The expectations of society, based on traditional wisdom and common sense, must bow before the autonomous individual. This way of thinking about identity, grounded in political ideology and claims regarding newly discerned rights and freedoms, becomes a substitute for thinking about the self in religious terms; its conclusions differ markedly from those of the religious vision of human nature and human life. The self in political ideology exists over against others instead of in communion with them. Moreover, such an identity is grounded solely in the physical, which is the vehicle of a consciousness that can only have emerged from material reality and thus have only a material cause. To this way of thinking, it is material reality that must be perfected, in the process itself becoming a commodity displayed in the digital world. However, the management of the digital, correlative self through the presentation of images of "my perfect life" fails to heal the wound of imperfection; the responsibilities placed on the autonomous self are unsustainable, and the result is loneliness, isolation, and — often — despair. Ultimately, the world of autonomous identities is unstable and sterile, and the sense of imperfection and incompleteness should thus be addressed in a different way, through an understanding of vocation.

Vocation is the call from outside of our selves to that loss of self that is our true life. As Peter Tyler has put it: "The fundamental question for the person discerning their vocation is that of St Benedict (and indeed the Psalmist): 'Is there anyone here who yearns for life and desires to see good days?'.... Essentially seeking advice on vocation is seeking advice on how to live a fulfilled and happy life."[5] In order to have right relationships with others, we do indeed need a right understanding of our own self and who we are called to be: our identity is hidden in the sometimes mysterious workings of our vocation. This is the insight of St John Henry Newman's famous meditation: "I am created to do something or to be something for which no one else is created."[6] Our right relationship with God is the source of our understanding of who we are to be: we are not autonomous beings but find ourselves in the Lord's service: "God has created me to do him some definite service; he has committed some work to me which he has not committed to another. I have my mission — I may never know it in this life, but I shall be told it in the next."[7] Our vocation may never be entirely transparent to us, and it also includes — and never removes — our woundedness: "If I am in sickness, my sickness may serve Him; if I am in sorrow, my sorrow may serve Him. My sickness, or perplexity, or sorrow may be necessary causes of some great end, which is quite beyond us."[8] To understand our woundedness within our vocation is to be able to come to a happy and fulfilled life in that woundedness, rather than in spite of it.

It would be some way wide of the mark to imply to the young that the promise of their education is worldly success. (Note the words of Thomas Merton quoted in Chapter 3.) Either success or failure, in worldly terms, might be the consequence of living out our vocation. An education that assists the young in finding their

---

5   Peter Tyler, "The Psychology of Vocation," in *The Disciples' Call*, ed. Christopher Jamison (London: T&T Clark Bloomsbury, 2013), 212.

6   John Henry Newman, *Meditations on Christian Doctrine* I, 2 (1893). http://www.newmanreader.org/works/meditations/meditations9.html.

7   Ibid.

8   Ibid.

vocation will offer them "a sign of contradiction." This sign was powerfully articulated in 2010 by Pope Benedict XVI in his speech to young people at St Mary's University College, Twickenham:

> When we are young, we can usually think of people that we look up to, people we admire, people we want to be like. It could be someone we meet in our daily lives that we hold in great esteem. Or it could be someone famous. We live in a celebrity culture, and young people are often encouraged to model themselves on figures from the world of sport or entertainment. My question for you is this: what are the qualities you see in others that you would most like to have yourselves? What kind of person would you really like to be?[9]

Pope Benedict reminded his audience that the promise of worldly success is illusory if it is seen as an ultimate value:

> Having money makes it possible to be generous and to do good in the world, but on its own, it is not enough to make us happy. Being highly skilled in some activity or profession is good, but it will not satisfy us unless we aim for something greater still. It might make us famous, but it will not make us happy....The key to it is very simple — true happiness is to be found in God. We need to have the courage to place our deepest hopes in God alone, not in money, in a career, in worldly success, or in our relationships with others, but in God. Only he can satisfy the deepest needs of our hearts.[10]

This is a challenge to teachers engaged in the everyday reality of a school, where we promote success in examinations, sporting

9 Benedict XVI, Address to pupils at Twickenham (September 17, 2010). http://w2.vatican.va/content/benedict-xvi/en/speeches/2010/september/documents/hf_ben-xvi_spe_20100917_mondo-educ.html.

10 Ibid.

competitions and university entrance and the promise of employment in the world of the professions, business, the academy, and even the Church: we can never imply that such success is the central concern of a Catholic and Benedictine education, however much a degree of success in worldly terms makes for human flourishing. A successful career might emerge from our schooling, but it has a larger (and more realistic) purpose than appearing to guarantee an illusion.

In the first place, the school promotes and seeks to embody what Abbot Christopher Jamison has called "a culture of vocation."[11] To do so, the school needs to understand itself as a place which seeks to make sense for young people of their encounter with the transcendent. Such an encounter cannot be driven, determined, or guaranteed (and certainly not sold as a "pupil outcome"), but a Catholic and Benedictine education should seek to clear a space where the transcendental vision becomes possible. Peter Tyler has outlined the process of vocational discernment through an analysis of the Grail legend, as told by Chrétien of Troyes. A young man, whose name is later revealed as Perceval, leaves his widowed mother's home in springtime in the Waste Forest, armed with three spears. He sees five armed knights, whom he takes to be angels, having initially considered them devils. He desires to be like them, and is tutored by an elderly knight named Gurnemanz before making his journey to the Grail Castle. There, he fails to ask the crucial question, "Whom does the Grail serve?" This is the question which will heal not only the boy from his pain of loss and desire, but the whole court, including the Grail guardian himself—the Fisher King—said to have been wounded as a young man when he first encountered the Grail.[12] In Tyler's interpretation, the essential elements are that Perceval is without a father, has a transcendental vision of his identity as a knight, engages with an older guide, learns his name, and makes mistakes in his encounter with the divine, which is the Realm of the Grail. Tyler

11   Christopher Jamison, ed., *The Disciples' Call*, 3.
12   Ibid., 220–21.

very helpfully distills from the story of Perceval eight lessons for discerning vocation:

1. Vocation is "about living life to the full" and finding our place in the "Mystical Body of Christ."
2. Vocation evolves through interaction with Positive Role Models.
3. The process of discerning vocation is about discovering our name.
4. The source of vocation is close to the sources and education of desire.
5. Vocation guides are "archetypal" in that they represent the wider transcendent realm.
6. The interaction of the Guide and Seeker will evoke many levels of psychological transference and countertransference.
7. Humility, and learning to serve God, is at the heart of the discernment of vocation.
8. Discovering vocation is about articulating and stabilizing our fleeting and earth-shattering encounter with the Transcendent.[13]

Vocation is not only, then, the key to finding our identity (or discovering our name); it is also the grounding of right relationships and good living. Teachers are not so much careers advisers as vocational guides, and never more so than when they seek to behave as positive role models. Like Perceval, so many of today's young have no father and their mother is alone. The encounter with the transcendent, the Holy, mystery, or God comes in this wounded human life and must be worked out in relationships with others. Pastoral care in a Catholic and Benedictine school is a way of meeting the reality of imperfection in faith, hope, and love. The young will make mistakes, will fail, and will disappoint themselves and others. They will misunderstand their gifts and fail to take their opportunities. But the narrative arc of their story,

13   Ibid, 222.

as of Perceval and of Christ (the true Fisher King), is that they are called to life, and life to the full, in the fullness of the Beatific Vision. The transcendent vision brings the joy of what is possible for us in relationships with others through our essential relationship, which is with God.

SPIRITUAL LIVING

Catholic and Benedictine education provides a context for the Gospel call to discipleship: "Follow me, and I shall make you fishers of men," says Christ, the Fisher King. This is a call to service, in humility of spirit, a call that comes to both teacher and pupil. The cleared space of vision is the temple, the *templum*, but the school itself operates beside the temple, rather as a courtyard of the gentiles.[14] This is the place of pre-evangelization, and also of encounters with witnesses, who may then become guides. The encounter with the transcendent opens up the possibility of a spiritual way of living, and the encounter is also with desire itself: we find ourselves as ones who "yearn for life, and desire to see good days." St Benedict begins in man's natural desire to transcend his limitations, and his constant admonition is that we should not accept second-best. The paradox of man is that he is in and to a great extent of this world, but he can never be satisfied by it. A transcendental education exists, first, to awaken in the young a recognition of their desire and the nature of their restlessness. It is the reason they, like Perceval, leave their maternal home, and undertake their journey. As Julián Carrón has put it, this is a journey into reality, with which the young engage in relationship; such is the end of education itself: "So, again speaking to teachers and students, Pope Francis said that 'school educates us to the true, the good and the beautiful. All three go together. Education cannot be neutral. It is either positive or negative; it either enriches or impoverishes; it either makes a person grow or it oppresses him, it may even corrupt him.... A school's mission is to develop the

---

14 See *Reclaiming the Piazza: Catholic Education as a Cultural Project*, 91.

sense of the true, the good and the beautiful. And this happens through a rich journey."[15] Beauty awakens desire, so beauty is the way into a true regard for reality. Carrón continues:

> From where can we start again, then? From reality. But not a reality reduced to appearance, because otherwise we grow tired of it, it leaves us dry, it cannot capture us or interest us for an extended time. From reality in its entirety and strength of provocation. Reality arouses an interest by attracting us; it proposed itself above all through its beauty, as Jorge Mario Bergoglio said: "How many abstract rationalisms and 'extrinsicist' moralisms could be cured ... if we began to think of reality first as beautiful, and only later as good and true!"[16]

Teachers are witnesses to beauty, especially in the subject they teach, but also in the values they embody. Christian teachers are witnesses, too, to the workings of the Holy Spirit in their lives, a presence (or radiance) that also expresses itself in beauty — of life, of thought, of work. The attractiveness of role models awakens a desire for that which makes them attractive. Good teachers do not draw this attraction towards themselves but to that which they profess, which is an embodied reality, not merely appearance. In the world of appearances, images, and disembodied faces, the young frequently experience an apathy from which they can only be awakened through the witness of persons, a witness that comes through relationships. Real persons have authentic voices, and the young listen to the authentic, while rejecting what they hear as bogus. The vocation to holiness can only work through authentic witnesses, who are the means of a genuine encounter with the spiritual life; they work in humility, which, St Benedict reminds us, is living close to reality.

---

15   Julián Carrón, *Disarming Beauty: Essays on Faith, Truth and Freedom* (Notre Dame, IN: University of Notre Dame Press, 2017), 141.

16   Ibid., 141–2.

Rather like the Rule of St Benedict itself, the Catholic and Benedictine school seeks to provide an induction into the spiritual life,
or the life of the Spirit. This is not merely a quality of "interiority,"
or inwardness, an encounter with the self. As David Albert Jones
puts it:

> The word "spirituality," in a Christian sense, is the trans-
> forming effect of the Holy Spirit upon the person as the
> person makes his or her way to God by the way that is
> Christ. There are many and diverse patterns and examples
> of Christian spirituality, some more austere, some more
> imaginative, some more stable, some more informal, but
> all will include these fundamental elements: the Holy
> Spirit, the person of Christ, transformation, the spiritual
> way, that is, the journey on "pilgrimage" to God.[17]

There must be witnesses, guides, and companions on this journey,
and a variety of forms of worship and prayer will be presented by
and to the young as means of encounter. Such forms of worship
will include the Mass, but schools should not rely solely on the
pinnacle of liturgy, which may be remote from the actual spiritual
development of many young people, who frequently come from
homes of little or no religious practice. The testimony of witnesses,
and opportunities to "break out" into different forms of prayer,
adoration, or confession, may mean more to some young people
than the Eucharistic liturgy that assumes a level of commitment
not yet there. Residential retreats can also provide occasions for
powerful encounters with the Spirit, encounters which might be
life-changing awakenings.

The induction into the spiritual life is part of the education
of the heart that is central to the Benedictine tradition. While
Catholic schools do not neglect the education of the intellect, and
develop in the young a sense of the interplay between faith and
reason, unless the possibilities of the Christian life root themselves

17 Jones and Barrie, 69.

in the desires and affections of the young they are unlikely to endure. As Newman reminds us, no one can be argued into believing in God, however much reason can support the promptings of faith; it is in "heart speaking to heart" that the life of the Spirit reveals itself. In so many situations — formal, informal, sacred, secular — the encounter with teachers as witnesses to beauty, and to the presence of Christ in their lives, can be the occasion of spiritual growth in the young. Such encounters integrate the Catholic curriculum around its mission in ways that no written statement, program, or schema can hope to match. However much we consider Catholic education as a great and socially redemptive cultural project, we should remind ourselves that it is in the salvation of individual souls that the wider society will be redeemed.

CONTINUING THE HUMAN

What happens to young people when they leave the particular environment of the Catholic school for college, university, or workplace — assuming that they will be fortunate enough for their lives to develop in this way? Will they be able to act as a "leaven" or will they be submerged by the weight of a culture that has lost connection with its Christian roots? Will they change or will they be changed? The hope of an education in spiritual living is that young people will find the sources of their life in God rather than the world, however much the world makes its impression on their life, especially through cultural norms. Increasingly, the culture around them seems to oppose itself to religion, so that it becomes more difficult for the rising generation to be open about any faith they may have. It is not impossible, however, to consider how the young may effect a change in cultural norms by living their lives vocationally, and with a sense of purpose. Quantitative judgments do not apply; the effect on relationships of a life lived well is incalculable, and the mission in a person's life, whether hidden or consciously understood, will be brought to fruition through trust in God's providential action. Nothing may be more important for the future health of the culture than that young people, on leaving school, live their lives according to the inherited norms of human nature — an inheritance they may need to recover and rediscover. One reason the young turn to religion and the way of the Spirit is that they see and feel in their own woundedness the social breakdown that has come from the neglect of the virtues and the pursuit of the self. Both the decline in religious faith and the return to it are the product of the decline of the family and all it represents and makes possible.

An authentic humanism, which the recent popes have promoted, is sustained by marriage and the family, yet these things have become marginalized among so many "life choices," and are not necessarily, in superficial terms, the most attractive. In that marriage and the family require an unconditional giving to others, they do not sit easily in a consumer society with "I" at the center. If, however, marriage and the family are understood in vocational terms, they can be seen to sit at the heart of an authentic humanism. A spiritual way of living makes possible a human flourishing in relationships with others; in turning away from the self, through a life of commitment to others, both "I" and "you" are transfigured by love. As St John Paul II showed us, and as Mary Eberstadt[18] has argued, the crisis of faith is bound up with the crisis of the family: both are in turn bound up with the crisis of humanism. Without the family, neither humanity nor faith can flourish: "The future of humanity passes by way of the family."[19] The Christian family as the basic cell of the Church is the family that St Benedict himself knew; it was the fundamental pattern of the early Church, coexisting with a culture with which it was at considerable variance: as many modern writers have suggested, this may also be a pattern for our times. Young people of faith may simply have to recognize that the way to their own human potential might put them at odds with the world around them,

---

18   See Mary Eberstadt, *How the West Really Lost God* (West Conshohocken, PA: Templeton Press, 2013).

19   John Paul II, *Familiaris Consortio* 86. http://w2.vatican.va/content/john-paul-ii/en/apost_exhortations/documents/hf_jp-ii_exh_19811122_familiaris-consortio.html.

in a culture that no longer reinforces or recognizes the norms of Christianity. Such a counter-cultural position will need an education in the virtues if it is to be sustainable.

Schools of various kinds, with varying senses of their own ethos, will commit themselves to the welfare, health, and well-being of their pupils — and, increasingly, their staff. This might involve attention to "mindfulness," forms of meditation, yoga, and advice on stress-reduction. Such approaches come out of a recognition that modern life brings peculiar pressures that need particular coping strategies. Mindfulness can bring with it some helpful meditative techniques, but insofar as it promises a withdrawal into the mind it may be simply another manifestation of a self-centered culture. At its deepest level, rooted in Eastern non-Christian religions, it may propose that the self is an illusion, and so mean the opposite of a full realization of personhood. Mindfulness may seem to offer the benefits of religion and spirituality in a secularized and pluralistic culture afraid of the effects of modern life on the mental health of the young: anxiety, depression, even suicide. But if mindfulness is about "taking control" of your own life, it is simply about playing the system very well: it is a symptom of modern ennui, disquiet, and pointless activity, not a cure. In a Christian culture, the culture a Catholic and Benedictine school should foster, meditation techniques need to be a part of a culture of prayer which in "lifting the heart and mind to God" takes us out of ourselves into the life of a Person who in turn gives life to our own personhood. The only lasting answer to questions of mental and physical health in the pupils and staff of a Catholic and Benedictine school will be found in the Gospel, alongside helpful cultural manifestations of the Gospel in the Christian monastic tradition.

We have said before that the Rule of St Benedict is distinguished by its humanity, deriving directly as it does from Roman notions of *humanitas*. We have also seen how St Benedict and his Rule have reappeared in our cultural and religious consciousness as a developed idea of human potential at a time of crisis in civilization, education, and humanism. The Western culture that came out of Christianity—especially monasticism—no longer takes its reference points from Christianity, and may be hostile to it. Yet the humanism of St Benedict's Rule is still highly attractive in non-religious contexts such as business, as well as schools. The ABCU Ten Core Values of a Benedictine Community[20] also provide a guide for family life, the basic community in which personhood develops in relationships with others. Personhood is to be desired and to be hoped for: this should be a school's message to the young. A life of moderation, balance, trust, and fidelity allows the human person to flourish and to be sustained amid life's vicissitudes. The spiritual life brings with it the moral life that is the only real guarantor of a measure of health in a world of woundedness and imperfection. The only kind of perfection we can hope for is "hidden with Christ in God." The integrated life brings with it in its realism the ability to face death, which, as various Benedictine educators have quipped, is what a Benedictine education prepares the young for.

---

20   A reminder: Love, Prayer, Stability, *Conversatio morum*, Obedience, Discipline, Humility, Stewardship, Hospitality, and Community.

CONCLUSION

A JOURNEY INTO SPACE

Walter M. Miller, Jr. was one of the American servicemen who took part in the bombing of Monte Cassino in 1944. It was a traumatic experience for him. After the war, Miller became a Catholic, and also a writer of science-fiction stories. Some of his stories eventually became his most successful work, a novel called *A Canticle for Leibowitz*, published in 1959. In the novel, Miller imagines three future periods that span a time from a twentieth-century nuclear conflict to a thirty-seventh-century journey into space. Each of the three parts of the novel centers on a community of monks of the fictional Albertian order of St Leibowitz, who have managed to preserve learning through a dark age that followed a nuclear war in the twentieth century. In the third part, once mankind has rebuilt civilization and technology, the Leibowitzan monks are about to leave the earth, now on the verge of another nuclear conflagration, to take learning and humanity to another world. In this dystopian and apocalyptic vision, the Catholic Church and monasticism have endured; civilization falls, but rises again through the enduring existence of monasticism. History is cyclical, but something seems permanently left behind as the thirty-seventh-century monks are about to leave a world determined to destroy itself. In a sense, the monks are leaving humanity itself behind, and journeying into a post-human future, on the threshold of space and a possible new world.

Science-fiction reflects a postmodern cultural sense of being on the threshold of a radically new human departure; the dark emptiness of space may also reflect the nothingness of the postmodern abyss, where there is no *logos* — no sense and no God. In *A Canticle for Leibowitz*, the journey at the end of monks and others (including children) to find a new Eden among the stars can be read as both the end of humanity (being swallowed up in an apparently irreversible nuclear apocalypse) and an image of renewal. Technology may be the death of us, and also the means of our survival. The monks in the novel preserve learning through an Age of Simplification, in which society at large, under the secular state, has rejected books as the source of evil. Other dystopian visions, such as Ray Bradbury's *Fahrenheit 451* (1953) and Margaret Atwood's *The Handmaid's Tale* (1985), also imagine a future in which the suppositions of the myth of progress are reversed. Insofar as dystopias reflect current cultural anxieties, such visions extrapolate from a perception that our culture has somehow turned against knowledge and learning as, by turns, either elitist or degenerating. It is a manifestation of the crisis of humanism, which since the Renaissance has seen learning as integral to the understanding of man as a rational creature in whom knowledge is a way to wisdom. In postmodernity, such a vision may be unraveling amid a fundamental skepticism regarding the validity of knowledge and the possibility of wisdom. Technology has also become detached from ethical certainties, to take on a life of its own. It is in this cultural context that we see the emergence of ideas of the *post-human*.

C.S. Lewis, writing during the Second World War, also anticipated a near future in which the decay of learning and its institutions would lead to the end of man as he has been known in the Classical and Christian West. In *The Abolition of Man* (1943), Lewis anticipates the consequences of a departure from traditional notions of natural law and a system of education that departs from moral objectivity. If education ceases to educate the heart as the unifier of the head and the visceral (animal) parts of our nature, society will be made up of "men without chests," who are more likely to be controlled by an elite minority purporting to possess a scientific, rationalistic understanding of what is best for everyone else. Lewis also explored the dehumanizing effects of a crisis in the purposes of learning, and in the "Old Western" understanding of human nature, in his science-fiction trilogy, in particular the third volume, *That Hideous Strength* (1945). Its contemporary setting is a college of medieval foundation that is divided about whether to develop modern, useful subjects such as sociology or keep to older subjects, like classics, that educate the heart and mind. A state organization takes over the college and through it alien invaders seek to take over the world. The aliens turn out to be demonic beings. On one level, the novel ("a fairy tale for grown ups" as Lewis subtitles it) is an exploration, in imaginative terms, of how the controllers and the controlled may become less than human, and the post-human future becomes a dystopian hell. The promise of a technological super-humanity will become a pact with the devil, and the price will have been the human soul.

A POST-HUMAN FUTURE?

More recently, Francis Fukuyama has explored in non-fictional and philosophical terms the possible results of the effect of technology on human nature. In *Our Posthuman Future: Consequences of the Biotechnology Revolution* (2002), Fukuyama begins with a review of *Nineteen Eighty-Four* (1949) and *Brave New World* (1932), by George Orwell and Aldous Huxley respectively. Both of these dystopian novels anticipate the destruction of learning, literature, and language (all three the means of transmission of a humane culture) as a part of political projects to destroy human nature as it has been traditionally understood. Orwell's vision is of destruction through pain, Huxley's through pleasure, and between themselves they capture two sides of the dehumanizing effect of ideology and technology in the twentieth century. Like C. S. Lewis, they envisage a world in which the aim is to destroy the heart of man, his capacity for love, affection, sentiment, and courage, and thus humanity itself. Fukuyama's central concern is whether it will be possible to make ethical and political steps to control what technology may enable us to do in the fields of genetic engineering, neuropharmacology and the control of behavior, and the prolongation of life; if we cannot control what we are becoming able to do, what will be the effect on human values as expressed especially in the cultures and politics of liberal democratic societies? What will be the consequences for human rights, human nature, and human dignity?

Fukuyama neither accepts nor rejects the religious conclusions on human nature as expressed in the Judeo-Christian tradition, but he takes them seriously. Indeed, his considerations of what constitutes human nature are not far from those of Christian apologists such as C. S. Lewis and St John Paul II:

> Human nature is what gives us a moral sense, provides us with the social skills to live in society, and serves as a ground for more sophisticated philosophical discussions of rights, justice and morality. What is ultimately at stake with biotechnology is not just some utilitarian cost-benefit calculus concerning future medical technologies, but the very grounding of the human moral sense, which has been a constant ever since there were human beings. It may be the case that, as Nietzsche predicted, we are fated to move beyond this moral sense. But if so, we need to accept the consequences of the abandonment of natural standards for right and wrong forthrightly and recognize, as Nietzsche did, that this may lead us into territory that many of us don't want to visit.[1]

It is now over fifteen years since Fukuyama's book was published, and longer still since the dystopian fictions of the mid-to-late twentieth century articulated the post-human future. From some perspectives, post-humanity is already with us, embracing all those possibilities expressed in the *trans-* words, *transgender* and *trans-human* especially. The essential concern, from the religious perspective, is whether the possibilities of technological intervention into human biology, combined with the lack of education, in learning and wisdom, of the human heart, will lead to the death of the human soul.[2]

---

1 Francis Fukuyama, *Our Posthuman Future: Consequences of the Biotechnology Revolution* (London: Profile Books, Ltd., 2003), 101–2.

2 On the philosophical antecedents, and religious nature, of transhumanist thinking itself, see John Gray, *Seven Types of Atheism* (London: Allen Lane, 2018).

In the final analysis, one should not treat dystopian visions as bearing ultimate authority on the shape of the future. Reality can be both more terrible in some ways and less so in others; it is certainly never quite so coherent, so total, as to eradicate "the last man," as in Orwell's vision. The extremes of genetic engineering and of artificial intelligence such that (for example) a complete separation of body and mind can be effected would only likely ever affect a tiny proportion of the human population. The totalitarianism of twentieth-century dystopias has been made less possible, rather than more so, by the digital revolution of the early twenty-first century; while the internet has increased the potential for state surveillance, it has also enabled greater freedom of communication between individuals. Nonetheless, if the idea of the human soul, as something sacred and beyond matter while also existing fully within the physical realm, vanishes from human consciousness, people will live as if their own soul and the souls of others have no existence. It could be agreed, in this sense, that the post-human world has arrived for many in our world, as the sacred and the transcendent disappear from view. However firm our trust in technology as the vehicle to the heavens, it is only a power failure away from a death of its own. In such a possible future, an Age of Simplification as Walter M. Miller put it, we shall have much need of the virtue of hope:

> Hope is the virtue associated with looking with confidence to one's ultimate end. Hope is what enables us to persevere, even under adversity. Hope also helps us maintain a focus on what the end requires, ignoring temptations that will ultimately frustrate our progress. And temptations will certainly abound in our posthuman future. Thus, we must become, as the prophet Zechariah (9:12) put it, "prisoners of hope" who forgo heaven on Earth to enter into union with God.[3]

3 James F. Caccamo, "The Catholic Tradition and Posthumanism: A Matter of How To Be Human," in *Posthumanism: The Future of Homo Sapiens* (Farmington Hills, MI: Macmillan Reference USA, 2018), 201.

It would be more human to be prisoners of hope than to be prisoners of the machine.[4]

THE ENDURING GOSPEL

A Catholic and Benedictine education for the future should be one that includes training in the virtues, as well as the arts and sciences, so that people can continue to find a freedom that does not destroy human nature and human potential. An education of the mind and heart, of the body and the soul, will be an integrated vision of who man is and who he is called to be. Such an education opens a vision of the goodness, truth, and beauty of reality, such that a life in the Gospel is possible. The Rule of St Benedict is about how to live the Gospel in the reality, both personal and communal, of human nature. Arts and sciences, including the means of wise intervention in nature (including one's own individual nature), are themselves products of human nature; man is a maker who can partly make himself. But unless he accepts that there is already glory in all things, were he able to see it, he is at risk of making reduced facsimiles of reality, idols that diminish him and bring death. Only wisdom (as opposed to skill or even knowledge), St Benedict's way of humility, provides a way to see things as they really are: this is the promise of a true education, and the way in which the young can come to an understanding of themselves and the world around them. The Gospel preserves all this for the future. As Christ said, "Heaven and earth will pass away, but my words will never pass away." In the mutability of all things, the Gospel remains.

---

4   In *Homo Deus* (2016), the recent bestseller by Yuval Noah Harari, the machine has become the algorithm, and organisms (including humans) are carbon-based, as opposed to silicon-based, algorithms. Harari argues that humanism (meaning the man-centered, post-Enlightenment world) will soon collapse to make way for a machine-driven search for human immortality, eternal happiness, and divinity. Man will disappear in this possible future, although some superhumans may emerge, bearing similarities with the controllers in C. S. Lewis's *The Abolition of Man*.

The prospect of radical disenchantment,[5] of a soulless world, is one that has haunted modernity. On the human level, this is the prospect of an impoverished life, a reduction of possibilities that can meet man's desire and his need to live well, to live a life worth living. The promise of a fully humane education, however, is that the Gospel reveals a radiance at the heart of things, a glorious shining, the uncreated light of the *logos* which is the opposite of the postmodern abyss: there is no emptiness. This is the true light that the Enlightenment threatened to banish, and in fact, for many, did cast into shadow. Education, therefore, must recover things from the pre-modern world where St Benedict lived in order to see again the glory that abides in all things. This is not to suggest that the way of St Benedict is intrinsically the greatest or in any sense a *sine qua non*: there is no Benedictine way without the Gospel. But the Rule of St Benedict is a valuable resource for Catholic education in reminding us of something that was diminished even in the Church in modernity, and that is the reasons of the heart of which the reason knows nothing, to adapt Pascal, a very modern critic of modernity. Human desire reaches beyond reason, which in itself is limited (this is perhaps the only truth glimpsed in postmodern thought). A true education of desire, of what one wants from life, is an education with the Gospel and Christ at the center. The Rule of St Benedict provides a real-world picture of what such a life might look like, a model for living with our own self and with others.

The Christian realism of the Rule of St Benedict provides a useful alternative to the utilitarian realism that possesses much modern educational thought, where outcomes for pupils are measured in terms of public exam results and benchmarks from competitor schools, league tables and standardized tests. Such systems cannot determine, however, what is taught and how, since they suggest there is no point in learning what cannot be measured. With a right sense of utility, properly and fully understood, we might ask:

---

5   By contrast, see Stratford Caldecott, *Beauty for Truth's Sake: On the Re-enchantment of Education* (Grand Rapids, MI: Brazos Press, 2009).

what's the use, in relation to a human person's true end? This may be the most up-to-date question concerning education, as employers turn back to the qualities of the person before them, not the vitiated qualifications recorded on a *curriculum vitae.* It seems at times that society recognizes, at the deepest level, that there is no substitute for a person possessed of a virtuous character, capable of commitment and love, and with a supple intellect that values the good, the true, and the beautiful. However much the culture works against such a consciousness, it may be that submerged human nature endures, awaiting recognition. It is the responsibility of education, in the meantime, to provide for such new times.

ACKNOWLEDGEMENTS

This book has grown out of years of friendship with St Benedict, his *Rule*, and many Benedictines, both living and dead. In addition, many fruitful discussions with many lay colleagues and pupils over many years have also contributed to my understanding of St Benedict. To both religious and lay friends, I acknowledge a debt of gratitude.

I am indebted also to teachers in my childhood and youth, Marist sisters and Presentation brothers, who lived religious lives of dedication, service, and prayer. They preached the Gospel in their kindness and wisdom, and provided a pattern of what the religious life might mean.

I am especially grateful to Dom Martin McGee, a monk of Worth Abbey, who kindly and patiently offered detailed comment on the manuscript, and amplified my understanding and treatment of the important Benedictine quality of stability. I am also very grateful to my friend Ian Crowe of Belmont Abbey College, North Carolina, for the opportunities he gave me to talk to students and faculty about this book.

Many of the ideas here have been developed in recent conversations with colleagues at Worth, and in the context of our leadership conferences, and I am grateful to everyone, from here and elsewhere, with whom I have had the privilege to discuss the nature of what we do in the education of the young. I am especially grateful to Stuart McPherson, Head Master of Worth School, for his support of this and my other formation projects.

Parts of Chapter 1, "Beginnings," appeared in an article in the *Catholic Herald* on September 5, 2014.

I am very grateful to John Riess of Angelico Press for his unfailing support and guidance.

Most of this book has been written in time eked out of school vacations, and as such has required the patient understanding of my family, from whom also I have received much inspiration.

Turners Hill, Sussex.
November, 2018

BIBLIOGRAPHY

American and Canadian Association of Benedictine Colleges and Universities, The. "Education within the Benedictine Wisdom Tradition." https://www.abcu.info/index.asp?SEC=94EFD1ED-B758-49CE-A3EA-1688AFFC9AC7&DE=47641124-0236-45D2-9FD4-2B0617CC3C1A.

Barry, Patrick. *Saint Benedict's Rule*. Santiago, Chile: Editorial San Juan, 2004.

Belloc, Hilaire. *Europe and the Faith*. Rockford, IL: TAN Books, 1992.

Benedict XVI, Pope. Address to the Participants in the International Congress Organized to Commemorate the 40th Anniversary of the Dogmatic Constitution on Divine Revelation *Dei Verbum*. Castel Gandolfo, September 16, 2005, http://w2.vatican.va/content/benedict-xvi/en/speeches/2005/september/documents/hf_ben-xvi_spe_20050916_40-dei-verbum.html.

——. Address to pupils at Twickenham, September 17, 2010. http://w2.vatican.va/content/benedict-xvi/en/speeches/2010/september/documents/hf_ben-xvi_spe_20100917_mondo-educ.html.

——. *Deus Caritas Est*. http://w2.vatican.va/content/benedict-xvi/en/encyclicals/documents/hf_ben-xvi_enc_20051225_deus-caritas-est.html.

Berg, Stephen Thomas. "St Benedict's Enduring Rule." http://www.growmercy.org/wp-content/uploads/St.%20Benedict%27s%20Enduring%20Rule.pdf.

Bernard of Clairvaux. *Selected Works*. Translated by G. R. Evans. New York: Paulist Press, 1987.

Butler, Cuthbert. *Benedictine Monachism: Studies in Benedictine Life and Rule*. London: Longmans, Green and Co., 1919.

Caccamo, James F. "The Catholic Tradition and Posthumanism: A Matter of How To Be Human." In *Posthumanism: The Future of Homo Sapiens*. Farmington Hills, MI: Macmillan Reference USA, 2018.

Caldecott, Stratford. *Beauty for Truth's Sake: On the Re-enchantment of Education*. Grand Rapids, MI: Brazos Press, 2009.

——. *Beauty in the Word: Rethinking the Foundations of Education*. Tacoma, WA: Angelico Press, 2012.

Carrón, Julián. *Disarming Beauty: Essays on Faith, Truth and Freedom*. Notre Dame, IN: University of Notre Dame Press, 2017.

Castle, E. B. *Ancient Education and Today*. London: Penguin, 1964.

Catechism of the Catholic Church. http://www.vatican.va/archive/ENG0015/_INDEX.HTM.

Chesterton, Gilbert Keith. *The Everlasting Man*. London: Hodder and Stoughton, 1925.

—. *Heretics*. London: Bodley Head, 1905.

Collini, Stefan. *What Are Universities For?* London: Penguin, 2012.

Collins, Jim. "Level 5 Leadership: The Triumph of Humility and Fierce Resolve." In *On Leadership*. Boston, MA: Harvard Business Review Press, 2011.

Convery, Ronnie, Leonardo Franchi, and Raymond McCluskey. *Reclaiming the Piazza: Catholic Education as a Cultural Project*. Leominster: Gracewing, 2014.

—. *Reclaiming the Piazza II: Catholic Education and the New Evangelization*. Leominster: Gracewing, 2017.

Dawson, Christopher. *Christianity and European Culture: Selections from the Work of Christopher Dawson*. Edited by Gerald J. Russello. Washington, D.C.: CUA Press, 1996.

Demacopoulos, George E. *Gregory the Great: Ascetic, Pastor and First Man of Rome*. Notre Dame, IN: University of Notre Dame Press, 2015.

Dollard, Kit, Anthony Marrett-Crosby, and Timothy Wright. *Doing Business with Benedict: The Rule of St Benedict and Business Management: A Conversation*. London: Continuum, 2002.

Dreher, Rod. *The Benedict Option: A Strategy for Christians in a Post-Christian Nation*. New York: Sentinel, 2017.

Eberstadt, Mary. *How the West Really Lost God: A New Theory of Secularization*. West Conshohocken, PA: Templeton Press, 2013.

Eliot, T. S. *The Complete Poems and Plays of T. S. Eliot*. London: Faber and Faber, 1969.

Foster, David. *Reading with God: Lectio Divina*. London: Continuum, 2005.

Frost, Robert. *The Poetry of Robert Frost*. New York: Holt, Rinehart and Winston, 1969.

Fukuyama, Francis. *Our Postmodern Future: Consequences of the Biotechnology Revolution*. London: Profile Books, 2003.

Galbraith, Craig S. and Oliver Galbraith. *The Benedictine Rule of Leadership: Classic Management Secrets You Can Use Today.* Avon, MA: Adams Media, 2004.

Gargano, Innocenzo. *Holy Reading: An Introduction to Lectio Divina.* Translated by Walter Vitale. Norwich: Canterbury Press, 2007.

Gaudium et Spes. http://www.vatican.va/archive/hist_councils /ii_vatican_council/documents/vat-ii_const_19651207_gaudium -et-spes_en.html.

Grace, Gerald. "Catholic social teaching should permeate the Catholic secondary school curriculum: an agenda for reform." *International Studies in Catholic Education* 5, No. 1 (March 2013).

—. *Faith, Mission and Challenge in Catholic Education.* Abingdon, Oxon: Routledge, 2017.

Gray, John. *Seven Types of Atheism.* London: Allen Lane, 2018.

St. Gregory the Great. *The Book of Pastoral Rule.* Translated by George E. Demacopoulos. Crestwood, NY: St Vladimir's Seminary Press, 2007.

—. *Life and Miracles of St Benedict.* Translated by Odo J. Zimmerman, O.S.B. and Benedict R. Avery, O.S.B. Collegeville, MN: Liturgical Press, 1949.

Grint, Keith. *Leadership: A Very Short Introduction.* Oxford: Oxford University Press, 2010.

Guardini, Romano. *The End of the Modern World.* Translated by Joseph Theman and Herbert Burke. Wilmington, DE: ISI Books, 1998.

—. *The Spirit of the Liturgy.* Translated by Ada Lane. New York, NY: Crossroad Publishing Co., 1997.

Hapgood, David and David Richardson. *Monte Cassino.* New York: Berkley Books, 1986.

Hayes, Michael and Liam Gearon, eds. *Contemporary Catholic Education.* Leominster: Gracewing, 2002.

Harari, Yuval Noah. *Homo Deus: A Brief History of Tomorrow.* London: Vintage, 2017.

Huizinga, Johan. *Homo Ludens: A Study of the Play-Element in Culture.* Kettering, OH: Angelico Press, 2016.

Jamison, Christopher, ed. *The Disciples' Call: Theologies of Vocation from Scripture to the Present Day.* London: T & T Clark Bloomsbury, 2013.

John Paul II, Pope. *Familiaris Consortio.* http://w2.vatican.va/content/john-paul-ii/en/apost_exhortations/documents/hf_jp-ii_exh_19811122_familiaris-consortio.html.

—. *Fides et Ratio.* http://w2.vatican.va/content/john-paul-ii/en/encycli-
  cals/documents/hf_jp-ii_enc_14091998_fides-et-ratio.html.

—. *Memory and Identity: Personal Reflections.* London: Phoenix, 2005.

Jones, David. *Epoch and Artist: Selected Writings.* London: Faber and Faber,
  2008.

Jones, David Albert and Stephen Barrie. *Thinking Christian Ethos: The
  Meaning of Catholic Education.* London: Catholic Truth Society, 2015.

Kardong, Terrence. *Benedict Backwards: Reading the Rule in the 21st Century.*
  Collegeville, MN: Liturgical Press, 2017.

—. *The Benedictines.* Dublin: Dominican Publications, 1988.

Knowles, David. *The Benedictines.* Eugene, OR: Wipf and Stock, 2009.

—. *Saints and Scholars: Twenty-five Medieval Portraits.* Cambridge: Cambridge University Press, 1962.

Kuby, Gabriele. *The Global Sexual Revolution: Destruction of Freedom in the
  Name of Freedom.* Kettering, OH: Angelico Press, 2015.

Leclercq, Jean. *The Love of Learning and the Desire for God: A Study of Monastic Culture.* New York: Fordham University Press, 1982.

Le Mée, Katharine. *The Benedictine Gift to Music.* New York: Paulist Press,
  2003.

Lewis, C. S. *The Abolition of Man.* San Francisco: Harper Collins, 2001.

Lichtmann, Maria. *The Teacher's Way: Teaching and the Contemplative Life.*
  New York: Paulist Press, 2005.

Little, Tony. *An Intelligent Person's Guide to Education.* London: Bloomsbury, 2015.

Longenecker, Dwight. *Listen My Son: St Benedict for Fathers.* Leominster:
  Gracewing, 2000.

Lynch, Joseph H. *The Medieval Church: A Brief History.* London: Longman, 1992.

MacIntyre, Alasdair. *After Virtue: A Study in Moral Theory.* London: Duckworth, 1985.

Maredsous, Abbey of. *Benedictini Vivendi Praeceptores: Actes du Colloque
  de Pédagogie bénédictine.* Editions de Maredsous, 1981.

Marr, Andrew. *Tools for Peace: The Spiritual Craft of St Benedict and René
  Girard.* New York: iUniverse, Inc., 2007.

Merton, Thomas. *Thomas Merton: Spiritual Master: The Essential Writings.*
  Edited by L. Cunningham. New York, NY: Paulist Press, 1992.

Miller, Walter M. *A Canticle for Leibowitz.* London: Orbit Books, 1993.

Moore, Brian. *Catholics*. London: Vintage, 1992.

Newman, John Henry. "The Benedictine Schools." 1859. http://www.newmanreader.org/works/historical/volume2/benedictine/schools.html.

—. *Meditations on Christian Doctrine*. 1893. http://www.newmanreader.org/works/meditations/meditations9.html.

—. "The Mission of St Benedict." 1859. http://www.newmanreader.org/works/historical/volume2/benedictine/schools.html.

—. *Tract One*. Didcot, Oxon: The Rocket Press, 1985.

Newman, Richard. *Saint Benedict in His Time*. Abergavenny: Three Peaks Press, 2013.

Paul VI, Pope. *Pacis Nuntius*. http://w2.vatican.va/content/paul-vi/la/apost_letters/documents/hf_p-vi_apl_19641024_pacis-nuntius.html.

Ratzinger, Joseph. *Christianity and the Clash of Cultures*. Translated by Brian McNeil. San Francisco: Ignatius Press, 2005.

—. "On Europe's Crisis of Culture." Lecture, Subiaco, Italy, April 1, 2005. https://www.catholiceducation.org/en/culture/catholic-contributions/cardinal-ratzinger-on-europe-s-crisis-of-culture.html.

—. *The Spirit of the Liturgy*. Translated by John Saward. San Francisco: Ignatius Press, 2000.

Robertson, Duncan. *Lectio Divina: The Medieval Experience of Reading*. Collegeville, MN: Liturgical Press, 2011.

Scruton, Roger. *Beauty: A Very Short Introduction*. Oxford: Oxford University Press, 2011.

—. *The Face of God*. London: Continuum, 2012.

—. *On Human Nature*. Woodstock, Oxon: Princeton University Press, 2017.

Steiner, George. *Real Presences*. Chicago: University of Chicago Press, 1991.

Storr, Will. *Selfie: How We Became Self-Obsessed and What It's Doing To Us*. London: Picador, 2017.

Studzinski, Raymond. *Reading to Live: The Evolving Practice of Lectio Divina*. Collegeville, MN: Liturgical Press, 2009.

Tolkien, J. R. R. *On Fairy Stories*. London: Harper Collins, 2008.

Trasancos, Stacy. *Science Was Born of Christianity: The Teaching of Fr. Stanley L. Jaki*. The Habitation of Chimham Publishing, 2014.

Waugh, Evelyn. *Men at Arms*, London: Penguin, 1964.

—. *Unconditional Surrender*. London: Penguin, 1974.

—. *Work Suspended and Other Stories*. London: Penguin, 1982.

Weil, Simone. "Reflections on the Right Use of School Studies with a View to the Love of God." 1942. http://www.hagiasophiaclassical. com/wp/wp-content/uploads/2012/10/Right-Use-of-School-Studies-Simone-Weil.pdf.

Whitehead, A. N. *The Aims of Education and Other Essays.* London: Williams and Northgate Ltd., 1932.

Whittle, Sean. *A Theory of Catholic Education.* London: Bloomsbury, 2015.

Wolf, Notker and Enrica Rosanna. *The Art of Leadership.* Collegeville, MN: Liturgical Press, 2013.

ABOUT THE AUTHOR

ANDRÉ GUSHURST-MOORE is a graduate of Oxford University and, since 2003, has taught in Benedictine schools, previously at Downside and presently at Worth School, where he is Second Master. His work has appeared in a number of periodicals in the UK and the US, such as the *Catholic Herald, Political Science Reviewer, University Bookman,* and *Chesterton Review.* He is the author of *The Common Mind: Politics, Society and Christian Humanism, from Thomas More to Russell Kirk* (Angelico Press, 2013). He is married with three grown children, and lives in West Sussex, England.

Printed by Amazon Italia Logistica S.r.l.
Torrazza Piemonte (TO), Italy